DuBay & Maire, Ltd.
445 North Wells Street
Suite 200
Chicago, Illinois 60611

Telephone: 312.222.0445
Facsimile   312.222.1450

CLASSICAL FURNITURE

Classical Furniture

David Linley

Harry N. Abrams, Inc., Publishers

TO MY MOTHER AND FATHER

Designed by Bernard Higton
Text Editor: Elizabeth Wilhide
Picture Researcher: Jenny de Gex

Library of Congress Cataloging–in–Publication Data
Linley, David. 1961–
    Classical furniture / David Linley.
        p.   cm.
    Includes index.
    ISBN 0–8109–3188–5
    1. Furniture — Styles.   2. Furniture, Classical.   I. Title.
NK2235.L56   1993
746.2—dc20   93–603

Published in 1993 by Harry N. Abrams, Incorporated, New York
A Times Mirror Company

First published in 1993 by Pavilion Books Limited, London

Printed and bound in Italy

CONTENTS

Jewellery box by David Linley Furniture, 1993

FOREWORD

My craftsman grandson has asked me to introduce this handsome book and nothing could give me greater pleasure than to do so with these few words. Over the years I have witnessed his progress as a furniture designer and maker and have greatly enjoyed watching an idea take shape from sketch to finished article. He has an unerring eye and a keen sense of design and this has been put to great effect in producing some wonderfully original, yet 'classical' furniture.

Classical furniture holds a special fascination for so many people. Elegant, beautifully proportioned, yet practical too, the furniture produced by the great craftsmen and designers of the eighteenth century remains as appealing today as it was when it was first created.

If every picture tells a story, a piece of furniture speaks volumes about the age in which it was made, the people who commissioned and eventually used it and those whose skills went into its execution. As a collector, I have, in a small way, come to appreciate the unique insight into the past such pieces can offer us.

It is especially heartening to see the classical tradition brought up to date in the work of young designers. A new generation has discovered the timeless appeal of classical design and in these endeavours, and others like them, a spirit of craftsmanship is kept alive and flourishing.

H. M. QUEEN ELIZABETH THE QUEEN MOTHER

INTRODUCTION:
REVIVAL OF AN ART

Nothing is truly elegant but what unites use with beauty.' This quotation, taken from an eighteenth-century play by Oliver Goldsmith, expresses an eternal principle of design. In the first century BC, the Roman architect Vitruvius listed three conditions that all good buildings should fulfil, best known in their sixteenth-century translation as 'commodity, firmness and delight'. Influenced by classical principles, 'beauty' and 'use' became the twin concerns of eighteenth-century designers, architects and craftsmen; while over a century later, the same ideas resurfaced in another context in the form of William Morris's famous 'golden rule': 'Have nothing in your houses which you do not know to be useful or believe to be beautiful.'

In the twentieth century design has often seemed to be exclusively concerned with function, practicality and use, at the expense of the other half of the equation. Previous generations appear to have had an instinctive sense of what was pleasing to the eye, and a confidence in their aesthetic judgements which we have lost.

The common ground for thousands of years was classicism, a powerful system of relating human experience and the natural world to the design of everything built, made and used. The world has changed, perhaps for good, and it is unlikely that the conditions that allowed such a consensus of opinion to exist will arise again. But if many designers today are returning to classical principles and ideas, it is because they believe, as I do, that it is a tradition well worth keeping alive.

Opposite: With inlays of harewood and Swiss pear, the sycamore spectacle case, holding 250 pairs,
was designed and made for Elton John by David Linley Furniture.
Above: Furniture-making unites craftsmanship and design, and provides the opportunity to work with one
of the most challenging natural materials.

This book provides an introduction to classicism as it applies to the design of furniture, particularly furniture from the eighteenth century. Both the period and the subject area have been described in formidable detail in many scholarly works littered with names, dates and terminology. My intention, however, is to give an impression of a great movement in design from the point of view of someone working in the field and inspired by the same ideas.

My interest in craftsmanship and design goes back to childhood days when my father rather unconventionally encouraged us to make our own toys and play-

Rolltop desk made by Röentgen, from the Royal Collection at Windsor Castle.

things. His great visual sense and the stimulating atmosphere of experiment in the design world of the 1960s were early inspirations. The flamboyant theatrical and interior designs of my great-uncle Oliver Messel were also influential, particularly in their unerring sense of proportion.

My father and I share a passion for how things work, which in my case took the form of a schoolboy fascination with machines and mechanical contraptions. In the same spirit, a favourite piece of furniture is a desk in the Royal Collection at Windsor; made by Röentgen, the desk has a rolltop front that slides up at the lightest touch and an intricate system of counterbalanced weights, altogether a superb example of precision and ingenuity in craftsmanship. And one of my own treasured possessions is a whatnot bought recently at a country house sale in Lincolnshire. Like many pieces of early nineteenth-century furniture, it is mechanical: push down on the top shelf and the three tiers compress in the middle to form a side table. The mechanism is so neat and concealed I am still not precisely sure how it works.

At Bedales, where I went to school, there was the progressive notion, still rare in education, that making things was the equal of academic achievement. The sheer pleasure of being in a workshop and the enthusiasm of the design teacher David Butcher led me eventually to study at Parnham House, the school of design and craftsmanship founded by one of the most famous names in modern English furniture, John Makepeace. At Parnham, I was lucky to be taught by Robert Ingham, in my opinion one of the best makers in England.

On the first day at Parnham, we were given sand-

Traditional marquetry techniques: Jack Wilde, one of our craftsmen, who once worked on the fitting out of the 'Queen Mary'.

paper and new planes, and instructed to rub the bases of the planes until perfectly flat. The body of a plane should lift the wood up smoothly; if the blade is uneven and chatters, the wood will be gouged. Blades used to be cast and then left to temper for three months, a standard of tool-making to accommodate the needs of the craftsman who could expect to use a plane every day of his working life. Now blades are not flat because they are no longer tempered, and planes and other hand tools are designed for only occasional use by weekend enthusiasts and hobbyists. The first lesson at Parnham was a powerful introduction to the demands of craftsmanship.

Another important lesson I began to appreciate was that, however eager one might be to show off newly acquired skills, sheer craftsmanship is not enough. Reacting against industrialized processes, many people come to see hand-making as an end in itself. It is easy to treat furniture-making as an excuse to display virtuoso techniques and forget all about design, but design and craft must work together to create a successful piece.

After I had finished the two-year course at Parnham, there was a period of several years spent first in a co-op and then in a small partnership, both based in Surrey. Our early efforts were often hit or miss and there were plenty of late nights chasing deadlines, but gradually commissions began to build up, and this work formed the genesis of David Linley Furniture, founded in 1985.

The company is dedicated to creating fine furniture in a modern classical idiom – traditional in its terms of reference rather than backward-looking or nostalgic. We use materials of high quality and employ skilled craftsmen to execute our designs; yet while many dif-

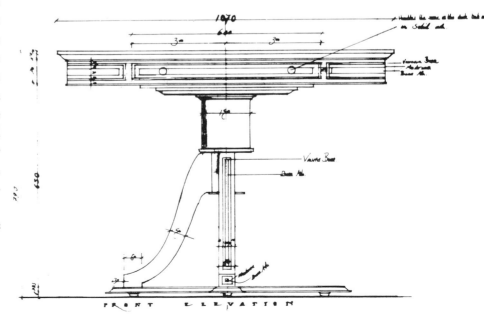

ferent specialists may work on a single piece, this does not mean we are opposed to the use of machines, where these do the job faster and more efficiently. But the main difference between a business geared to creating commissioned pieces, like our own, and a manufacturer producing bulk quantities of standard goods is that we do not have to limit a design to fit in with a machine process or a market profile, but can work closely with each client to produce unique items that reflect individual tastes and preferences.

Commissioned furniture is the result of a two-way process between the designer-craftsman and client. In the great age of furniture-making a large proportion of furniture was made to order; in fact, most things were. People commissioned houses, furnishings, clothes and pictures and took great pains to oversee the work in progress, getting involved with both choice of materials and elements of design.

The standard term for this system is patronage, a word which has unfortunate associations in a modern age. But patrons were not merely those with the wealth to acquire fine possessions; they participated fully in the creative process, stimulating new directions in design, enthusiastically promoting new ideas gathered on their travels and keeping a sharp and well-educated eye on standards. They took a long view. They expected the furniture they ordered and the houses they built to be used long after they were gone, and they were prepared to wait (sometimes impatiently) for the best.

Great eighteenth-century patrons, such as Lord Chesterfield, Thomas Jefferson and the Duke of Atholl, gained real pleasure from decorating and furnishing their houses. For many, it was a lifelong interest, almost an obsession. In the process, they may have spent substantial sums of money, but with certain exceptions not astronomical amounts. Yet in terms of time devoted to poring over designs, chivvying craftsmen and supervising work on site, it added up to a significant part of life.

Today the sheer pace of living has meant that few people are prepared to embark on the process of commissioning furniture when they can buy it direct from a showroom or department store. And short-term thinking breeds an unwillingness to invest in quality for the future. Nevertheless, it is clear from the growing number of publications on all aspects of the interior that we are just as interested in the way our houses look and what they contain as our ancestors were two hundred years ago, and we are still perfectly prepared to spend time, money and energy on our surroundings.

The true missing ingredient is confidence. Design has become the mysterious preserve of experts: even knowledgeable amateurs often feel excluded and unqualified to venture an opinion. As someone who would like to reverse this trend, I hope this book will provide a better understanding of what classical furniture, in particular, is all about and inspire readers to engage in the fruitful process of collaborating with a designer or craftsman to create a special piece of furniture for themselves.

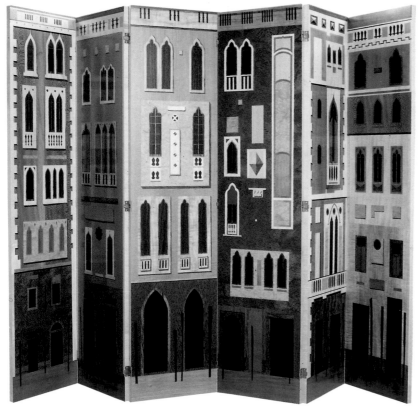

The glorious panorama of Venetian architecture was
the inspiration for one of the company's early successes,
the Venetian screens, and this painterly use of
marquetry has since become a trademark of David Linley
Furniture. Frank Lowe of the advertising agency
Lowe International bought one of the screens and went on
to commission a staircase for the London headquarters.
With parquetry steps predominantly in oak, the
stair portrays views of Venice in over 50 types of wood -
7,000 individual marquetry pieces.

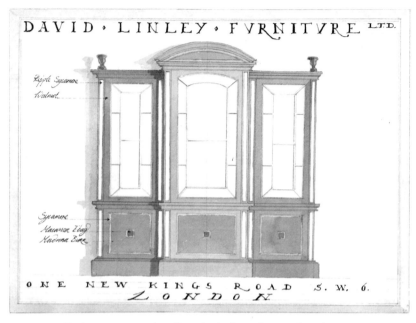

Designs are presented to clients in the form of watercolour drawings.

METHODS AND MATERIALS

A central pleasure of furniture-making is working with one of the finest of all natural materials: wood. Long-lasting, versatile, often richly coloured or beautifully patterned, the special characteristics of wood have been prized by craftsmen for many centuries. Unlike other natural materials, wood is incredibly varied, from species to species and even from board to board within the same tree. This diversity poses a challenge for those who work in wood, but it also reminds us wood comes from a living source.

There are estimated to be tens of thousands of species of timber grown around the world in temperate and tropical zones. But for furniture-making, there are probably fewer than thirty commonly used, and at any one time there are bound to be a few types of wood which are more popular than others, either because of their colour, grain or other qualities. The main distinction is between softwoods, which come from fast-growing evergreen trees with needle leaves, and hardwoods from deciduous trees, which are generally denser, more expensive, slower to mature and more varied in appearance as a group.

The history of furniture is often divided into periods which correspond to the different woods principally used at various times. In this way, the 'age of oak' gives way to the 'age of walnut', followed by the 'age of mahogany' and finally the 'age of satinwood'. Historians do not attach too much importance to such generalizations, but they do indicate changing styles and conditions.

Centuries ago, when northern Europe was covered in dense forests and oak was plentiful, wood was the principal material not only for furniture, but also for building. Oak was a natural choice for many different uses; it was readily available, strong, durable and easily split or 'cleft'. Yet by the seventeenth century, partly due to the expansion of shipbuilding, native stocks had already dwindled significantly and in 1666 the Great Fire of London provided a graphic illustration of the risks associated with timber construction. The trade in softwoods from Scandinavia and hardwoods from areas such as the West Indies grew in importance, while new legislation in the eighteenth century fostered the use of brick or stone, rather than timber in new houses.

We are at a similar crossroads today as it becomes clear that we can no longer carry on depleting the world's resources at will. Just as the oak forests of medieval England once seemed inexhaustible, until recently it was difficult to imagine that the world's supply of timber would ever run out. Furniture-making does not pose the greatest threat to the survival of world forests, but the impact is significant enough to demand a change in the types of wood we use. Hardwoods, because they take longer to replace, are most at risk.

If the great hurricane of October 1987 had a disastrous effect on the estates and public parks of Britain, the storm literally represented a windfall for British furniture-makers. The loss of trees was so great that much of the native hardwoods used in fine furniture in this country still come from the stock of fallen timber – oak, beech, elm, lime, ash and walnut being the most common varieties. But no one would wish to rely on

A range of furniture commissioned for St James's Court Hotel. The hall chair is in Swiss pear and Madrona burr, with ebony and harewood inlays on the back. The console table and Venetian mirror are both in sycamore, with Swiss pear and harewood inlays on the mirror frame.

such cataclysmic events for their supply of wood. Those involved in furniture-making today have the added responsibility of ensuring that their materials come from sustainably managed sources.

It takes time to become acquainted with different types of wood, their special characteristics and ease of working. Expertise in this area is a vital part of furniture design. Oak, for example, has an open, coarse grain but it is not especially easy to work or carve. Sycamore is a dense, smooth wood, almost white in colour; while walnut has a beautiful 'figure' or pattern of grain, but is structurally weak and prone to woodworm. Mahogany, as the craftsmen of the eighteenth century discovered, is an ideal furniture wood, dense, strong, worm-free

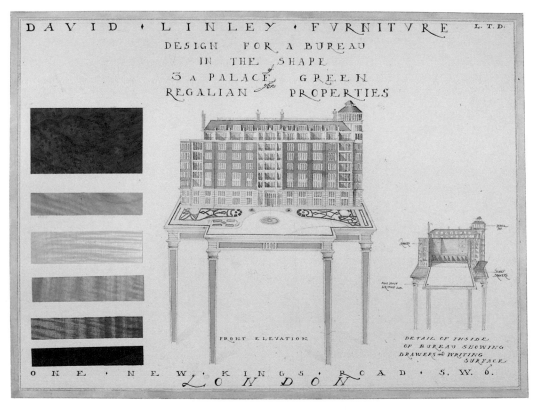

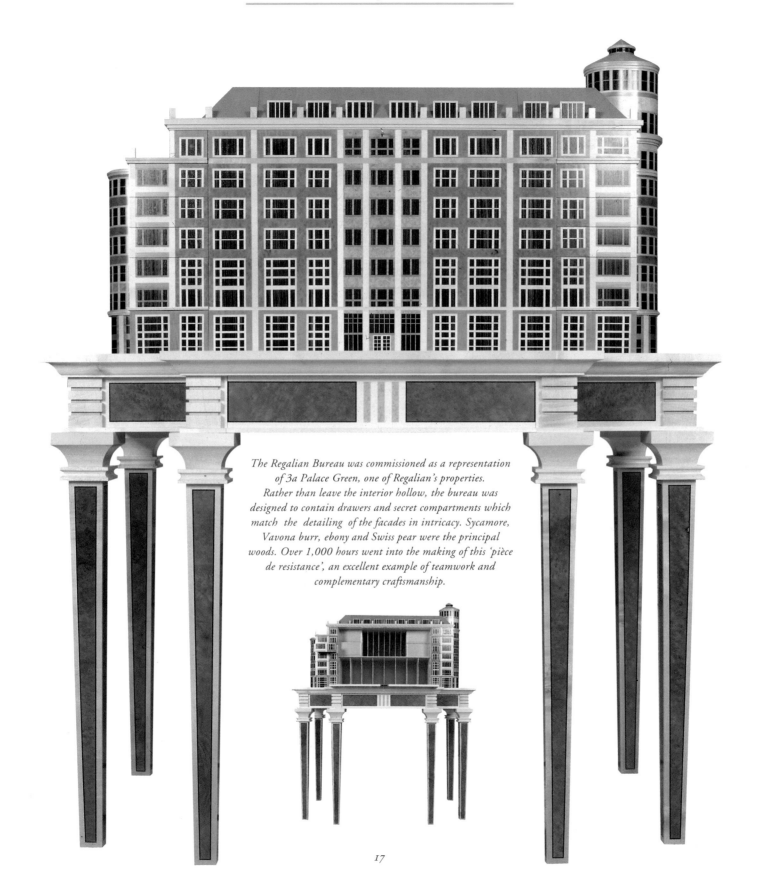

The Regalian Bureau was commissioned as a representation
of 3a Palace Green, one of Regalian's properties.
Rather than leave the interior hollow, the bureau was
designed to contain drawers and secret compartments which
match the detailing of the facades in intricacy. Sycamore,
Vavona burr, ebony and Swiss pear were the principal
woods. Over 1,000 hours went into the making of this 'pièce
de resistance', an excellent example of teamwork and
complementary craftsmanship.

and easy to carve. Hardwoods with the most exciting and vivid patterns are often those which are the weakest structurally and are best employed as veneers. Softwoods such as pine and deal are the traditional carcase materials, used for drawer linings, backs or underframes, or for cheaper types of furniture that would be covered up with a painted finish.

Another variable is moisture content. All wood contains a high proportion of water and, once a tree is felled, a percentage of moisture begins to evaporate until the wood reaches a point of equilibrium with the surrounding atmosphere. Managing this process is known as 'seasoning' or 'conditioning', and it can be carried out in many ways, including kiln-drying. Unseasoned or 'green' timber cannot be worked without running the risk of joints loosening as the wood shrinks, or panels cracking due to the tensions built up in the wood as it dries. Seasoned wood should ideally be worked in conditions which are not too dissimilar

Combining old with new, this design for a dining room table in ebony and maple features a glass top and pillar legs.

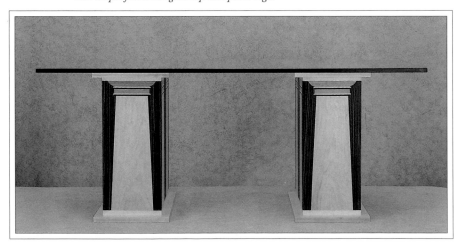

from those in which the finished piece will eventually be used.

Much of the furniture made by David Linley Furniture is in native English hardwoods, such as oak, sycamore and walnut, although walnut is proving increasingly hard to come by. As well as the classical nature of the designs, the use of marquetry has become something of a trademark, a facet of our work which began as a way of translating our watercolours into wood – literally, painting in wood.

Marquetry is a labour-intensive and meticulous discipline. Paper-thin veneers are cut to a design and pieced together before being applied to a solid base. With designs inspired by Venetian panoramas, the Wren churches of London and classical architectural details, our marquetry screens were an early success in this decorative idiom. One of the most elaborate commissions undertaken by the company was a staircase for the London headquarters of an advertising agency which incorporated 7,000 individual pieces of marquetry and 50 different types of wood. The parquetry steps were in three types of solid oak, while the side of the stairs consisted of marquetry views of Venice.

Our workshop near Cirencester, Gloucestershire, is the hub of a satellite operation which draws on the talents of many different freelance specialists, enabling us to combine traditional skills of hand-making with machine methods wherever these are appropriate. Machines are invaluable for professional furniture-making, but they make their own demands in terms of safety, noise, expense and disposal of waste. Whether hand or machine tools are used, the sequence of converting timber for use is roughly the same. First, the rough sawn board is cut to length and then to width (known as ripping). The next stage involves planing one face of the board to make a smooth flat surface, together with the adjacent edge. Finally, the board is dimensioned all round to a uniform thickness and width. There are a host of other operations, depending on the requirements of the design, including cutting mortises and tenons, cutting curves, profiling edges and turning round or shaped sections, not to mention the range of techniques involved in finishing. There are machines for each function, and machines which combine functions, but in fine furniture-making there are still many operations best left to the unique capabilities of hand tools.

Accurate and efficient working depends on thorough planning at the design stage. Whenever possible, the design process should be collaborative, with the client consulted at the very beginning of the commission for special requirements and preferences. It is vitally important to be aware, in particular, of the context in which the finished piece will be used and displayed, which can mean anything from the proportions of the room in question or the style of existing furniture to the type of items to be housed in a storage piece. Our work has been incredibly varied in scale and type. Among the largest pieces we have made was a 66-foot table for the Metropolitan Museum of Art in New York. Boardroom tables, reception desks and

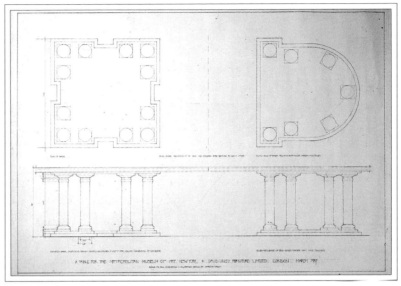

The 66-foot conference table for the Metropolitan Museum of Art, New York, is our single largest piece. Seating around sixty people, the table was conceived as a series of individual modules which could be used separately if required.

retail display cases are other commissions at this end of the scale, while smaller domestic pieces include jewellery boxes and a little drawered cabinet to keep a collection of pens. The opportunity afforded by such work to incorporate hidden compartments and secret drawers is one of the special pleasures of such individual commissions.

Furniture-making is uniquely satisfying. It demands a connoisseur's appreciation of materials, professional expertise in methods and techniques and the ability to respond imaginatively to the challenges posed by a wide variety of commissions. For most of us, meeting these standards is a life's work. The seemingly effortless skill and finesse of the great cabinetmakers of the past provides a constant source of inspiration.

CHAPTER ONE

THE CLASSICAL
IDEA

Classicism, in one form or another, has always been with us. With origins buried in antiquity, classical notions of proportion, symmetry and ornament have surfaced time and again in the history of design.

The ancient civilizations of Greece and Rome left an aesthetic legacy that shaped the entire course of Western thought. Principles of form and beauty, enshrined in great temples and civic monuments, set standards not only in architecture but also in the design, decoration and furnishing of interiors and the planning of landscapes and public spaces that were to influence architects and craftsmen for many centuries to come.

It was in Renaissance Italy during the fourteenth century that classical ideas were reborn and given new creative vigour. Ever since that time, classicism in one form or another has been a vital strand of design, a shared sensibility that links many of the world's greatest cultural landmarks, from the Pantheon to St Paul's Cathedral, from Palladian villas to the English country house. To understand the resilience of the classical spirit, it is important to examine its ancient beginnings and trace its growth.

Above: The Parthenon (447–432BC) in Athens expresses the purity of Greek classicism, a perfection of design that is nevertheless 'consummately human'.
Opposite: Timeless and exquisitely delicate, this three-legged Pompeiian table demonstrates the refinement of ancient Roman furniture.
Animal heads and feet were typical features of both chair and table design.

The Ancient World

The civilizations of Greece and Rome have been reinterpreted many times over thousands of years of history, in layers of discovery which serve to add their own complexities to the picture. And hindsight can also foreshorten our view of the ancient world, making a seamless strand of development out of the many different cultures which grew up, flourished, foundered and were lost. Over three thousand years separate the beginnings of Aegean civilization and the dying days of the Roman Empire: nearly two thousand more stretch from the defeat of Rome until the present day. Yet, despite the immense timescale, the uncertainties of historical research and the prejudice of other ages, classical notions of design remain a powerful and relevant source of inspiration.

In plain chronology, the Greeks came first and it was their 'orders' which the Romans copied and elaborated upon. But in terms of rediscovery, it was Roman architecture rather than Greek which provided the model for the architects of the Renaissance, and prompted the spread of classicism throughout the civilized world. For various reasons it was not until the eighteenth century that there was a classical revival which took direct inspiration from Greek architecture.

Classicism is sometimes characterized as a system of pure design concepts and aesthetic judgements, remote from earthier realities. But many critics believe that the origins of these basic orders of form and decoration lie in the natural world and man's relation to it, a fundamental connection which is at the heart of classicism's profound appeal.

This connection with nature is present at all levels.

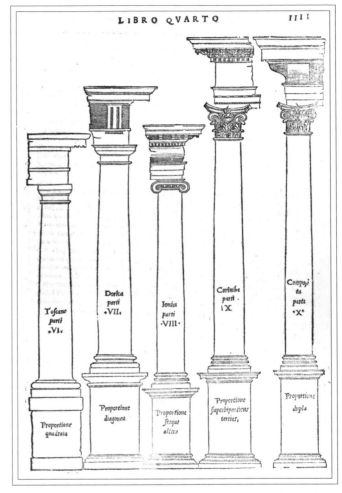

The five classical orders – Tuscan, Doric, Ionic, Corinthian and Composite – from Sebastiano Serlio's influential sixteenth-century treatise on architecture. Such publications spread the influence of classicism far and wide.

At the simplest, the basic forms of leaves, flowers, shells and animals are echoed in the stylized motifs of Greek and Roman decoration: the volute or spiral of the Ionic capital recalls ram's horns or nautilus shells,

The Composite order as reproduced in Sheraton's 'Drawing Book', 1791–4.
Eighteenth-century designers and architects made close study of the proportional details of each order.

The Tuscan order, from Sheraton's 'Drawing Book'.
The inclusion of the orders lent the appropriate air of classical
authority to pattern book designs.

placed on top. When Callimachus, a craftsman who worked in bronze, came across the basket, acanthus leaves had grown up to enclose it, curling under where they met the tile; Callimachus supposedly borrowed the flat-topped form with its curling leafy sides to create the Corinthian capital.

At a deeper level, Greek civilization was based on a highly organized system of nature worship where various elements were embodied by gods and goddesses. The rites and rituals associated with different deities were centred on the shrines and temples from which much of our knowledge of Greek architecture and design is derived.

The link with nature is also implicit in the way temples were constructed. The earliest buildings, religious and domestic, were made of wood. But even when translated into stone, specifically marble, the structure of Greek buildings retained the basic simple form of timber construction, known as 'trabeation' or post-and-lintel, where posts or uprights support beams on which the roof rests. Unlike the Romans, who developed domes and arched vaults, Greek buildings never progressed beyond this primitive structure of the hut. In the famous phrase, Greek architecture was 'carpentry in marble'. Marble was a particularly apt choice of material for rendering details first executed in wood, as it could be cut and worked with great precision and in superb detail.

The notion of 'orders' is central to classical architecture. There are three Greek orders, or systems of design: Doric, Ionic and Corinthian. Each order consists of vertical elements, the column, its base and capital and the horizontal elements (architrave, frieze and cornice) which make up the entablature. The earli-

the arching curls of the Corinthian capital are based on acanthus leaves.

One famous story illustrating the inspiration of nature was related by the Roman architect Vitruvius who made a systematic study of the classical orders in the first century BC. According to Vitruvius, the model for the Corinthian capital was a basket containing a devotional offering set down on top of a grave. To keep the contents of the basket safe, a tile had been

The massive amphitheatre of the Colosseum is a powerful example of the Roman use of the structural arch. This 1776 engraving by Piranesi dates from a time of intense interest in ruins and antiquities.

est, the Doric, shows very clearly the ancestry of timber building, with beam ends and wooden pegs copied in the details of the entablature. The Ionic was developed at much the same time as the Doric in a different part of Greece; while the Corinthian was later.

Ever since Vitruvius, the orders have been studied and catalogued minutely. But in broad terms, the orders show a process of proportional refinement accompanying an increase in decoration, with the Doric being the most robust and plain and the

Corinthian the most attenuated and embellished. The Ionic, with its spiral capitals and slender columns represents a midpoint between these two extremes. The different character of the orders meant that they have been traditionally associated with different uses.

The Greeks employed a number of corrective devices in the pursuit of elegance. Columns were slightly convex and tapering rather than straight to prevent them from looking narrow-waisted and weak. The outlines of horizontal elements such as cornices were also slightly convex so that they did not appear to sag in the middle. The upper lines of inscriptions running along the top of buildings had larger letters than the lower lines so that both would read the same size from below. There were many other highly sophisticated adjustments, both of structure and decoration, to accommodate the eye.

As Sir John Summerson has pointed out, one of the most important aims of classicism is to achieve 'a demonstrable harmony of parts'. Having a system of orders is one way of ensuring this. Another is to use simple ratios to generate a pleasing sense of proportion. The most familiar of these proportional relationships is the Golden Section, an aesthetic blueprint handed down to us from the Greeks. If a line is divided according to this ratio, for example, the greater length relates to the total in the same way as the shorter length relates to the longer. This ratio (phi or 1.618) has since been investigated by theorists working in many different fields. Their research appears to show that the ratio recurs again and again in the natural world, in the process of growth, in the spiral forms of shells and galaxies and in harmonic relationships in music, an eloquent testimony to the natural beauty of classicism.

The 'natural rightness' of the classical orders is evident to those who work with them. In *The Classical Language of Architecture,* Sir John Summerson quotes an illuminating passage in a letter written by the architect Sir Edwin Lutyens in 1903. Lutyens believed that the orders could not simply be copied, they needed to be understood so thoroughly it was as if each architect designed them anew. He wrote: 'When right they are curiously lovely – unalterable as plant forms. . . . The perfection of the [Doric] Order is far nearer nature than anything produced on impulse or accident wise.'

The Hellenic period (650–323BC) represents the high point of Greek civilization. Many of the most important temples were built in a space of barely fifty years following the defeat of the Persians at Salamis in 480BC. These include the supreme example of Greek temple building, the Parthenon (447–432BC), the temple to Athena built on the Acropolis in Athens. The Parthenon represents the finest example of the use of the Doric order; at the same time, the precision of the masonry is masterful. The elegance of both construction and design illustrates a striving for perfection and clarity. Architectural historian Sir Nikolaus Pevsner encapsulated the purity of Greek classicism when he wrote, of the Parthenon: '. . . there is something consummately human in all this, life in the brightest lights of nature and mind: nothing harrowing, nothing problematic and obscure, nothing blurred'.

While most of the important Greek buildings were temples, civic buildings such as theatres, meeting halls and tombs indicate how the orders could be used to create different kinds of structures. The considered layout of many public buildings, related to each other in symmetrical arrangements, show the principles of classical harmony applied on a wider scale.

The orders which the Greeks strove to perfect were eventually inherited by the Romans. To the original three, the Romans added the Tuscan (a squat, plain form of Doric), and the Composite, which combined Ionic volutes with elements of the Corinthian. Of all

Opposite: 'The Interior of the Pantheon' (1735) by Giovanni Paolo Panini (1691/2–1765).
The Pantheon, one of the greatest of all Roman architectural achievements, is the model of all classical
domed buildings. This vast interior is dramatically lit by one round opening.

Ceramic decoration has provided a lasting source of reference for the details of life in the ancient world. This Greek plate shows a man seated on a simple stool.

the orders, the Romans preferred the Corinthian; their version was more elaborately decorative than that of the Greeks.

The Tuscan order was taken from the Etruscan people who were early inhabitants of the western part of Italy. Also from the Etruscans, the Romans took the form of the arch. The Roman classical genius was to combine the design system of the orders with the new structural freedoms offered by arches and vaults. The orders were no longer structural but neither were they superfluous ornamentation: the means by which the orders were integrated with the structural elements gives the architecture its strength and power. The

results of this synthesis define our notions of classical architecture today.

The Colosseum in Rome is a key example. Multi-storeyed (Greek temples were single-storey structures), and with colonnades superimposed on the rows of structural arches, this massive amphitheatre shows how harmonious the integration can be. The Colosseum was a civic building. The diversity of building types, baths, amphitheatres, law courts, palaces and domestic blocks reflects the diversity of Roman society; while triumphal arches proclaim the glory of the Roman empire. Classicism, in the hands of the Romans, is wedded to authority and might but also richly varied in its range of applications.

The Pantheon, which comprises a domed cylinder with a projecting portico, displays Roman constructional skills at their height and is the model of all classical domed buildings. Implementing the principle of triangulation and exploiting the plasticity of concrete, the Romans were able to create the great vaulted spaces which were to have such an impact on the architects of the Renaissance.

It is hardly surprising that little furniture survives from the classical world. Yet, as eighteenth-century architects, travellers and connoisseurs were eventually to discover, ample evidence of the type of furniture in use in both ancient Greece and Rome is provided by sculpture, and in representations on pottery and wall painting.

Greek seat furniture ranged from four-legged stools braced with stretchers, or cross-legged, and couches with head and footboards for reclining, to more elaborate pieces such as the 'throne' chair and the klismos, an armless chair with curved legs and a shaped back

A Roman wall painting of Venus and Mars. As befits a goddess, Venus is seated in a grand armchair, embellished with carved detail.

rest. There were three-legged serving tables and chests for storage, but as yet no cupboards. Animal forms – especially feet and heads – were a feature of the finest pieces, as were inlays of ebony, ivory and precious stones, and carved and painted decoration.

Roman furniture was more varied and refined. Cross-framed stools were a common form of seating. A tub chair made of wickerwork was a typical woman's chair, while men sat on upright chairs with framed panels. The grandest chairs were armchairs, often decorated with animal reliefs. Couches had become more enclosed, sometimes with backs or sides. There was a greater range of table types, from great marble serving tables to small round tables with three or four legs. A new development was a type of console table, with curved legs and a semi-circular top. And there were the first cupboards, with shelves and doors.

THE RENAISSANCE

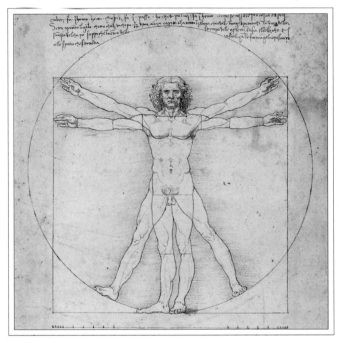

Vitruvian Proportional Man c.1487, by Leonardo da Vinci (1452–1519). To the Renaissance mind, classicism was the pure expression of the order and proportion of the natural world.

The legacy of ancient Greece and Rome took hundreds of years to uncover. Throughout the dark centuries of the Middle Ages, classicism lay dormant. It was not until the fifteenth century in Italy, more particularly in Florence, that these ideas began to be rediscovered.

The Renaissance represented a spectacular renewal of intellectual life, all the more remarkable because of the years of ignorance and turmoil that preceded it. Relative peace and stability in southern Europe and the rise of the confident mercantile class in the Italian city states provided the spur for an entirely new cultural direction. This is not to set aside the achievements of the Gothic cathedral-builders, an architectural tradition which remained deeply rooted in Northern Europe. But the Renaissance represented a profound break from the Gothic, replacing divine mystery with the clear light of human reason.

It is impossible in a short space to do more than to indicate the complex social and political events that fostered such a cultural upheaval; like many major movements in history, gathering forces of change found expression at the right place and the right time. With the Renaissance, classical ideas were not so much revived as reborn in the new climate of power and prosperity that characterized the city states of Florence, Rome and Venice.

The new movement had its origins in Florence around 1420. In 1425 Florentine artists rediscovered linear perspective and formulated it as a pictorial device; in 1450 the invention of printing enabled the spread of classical ideas of beauty and proportion. As the century progressed, the rediscovery of classical literature was the catalyst for a new artistic direction. Commerce flourished: the powerful banking family of the Medici (founded by Giovanni in 1424) were foremost among wealthy patrons who sponsored a glorious revival of art, architecture, painting and sculpture, all of which drew on classical precedents. Giovanni's son, Cosimo, founded the Medici Library and the Platonic Academy; his grandson, Lorenzo (the Magnificent) is synonymous with the most brilliant period of Renaissance Florence, a city of intense creative vitality. Our concept of 'Renaissance man', learned, well-versed in the arts and humanities, commercially successful yet creative, owes a great deal to the character of fifteenth-century Florence, with its almost modern notions of meritocracy.

Rome, the centre of the High Renaissance, did not display the same intermingling of disciplines as Florence. Nevertheless, important families such as the Malatesta and Este families, as well as aristocrats and the papacy encouraged the creation of a grand new city, filled with important buildings and embellished with sculpture and carving.

Venice, the third city state of this dynamic triumvirate, gained its wealth through trade. Nobles and merchants vied with each other in the creation of sumptuous palaces lining the Grand Canal, a panorama of architectural beauty unmatched in the world.

The model for this classical rebirth was Rome. Greece and its classical tradition were inaccessible: too far away and under foreign rule. Rome, however, was close at hand. Ruins were excavated and studied; and all too often plundered of building materials and decoration. Vitruvius' treatise on architecture, *De Architectura*, originally written in the first century BC but first published in 1486, was highly influential. Renaissance theorists, for whom Rome epitomized eternal beauty and artistic truth, saw the orders as holding the key to good architecture and set about devising rules for their implementation. Sebastiano Serlio recorded the five orders in a series of illustrated books, the first of which was published in 1537. The effect of such cataloguing was to set ideal standards of classical design to which architects referred for centuries to come.

Bramante's Tempietto of S. Pietro in Montorio, Rome, 1502, was built to commemorate the supposed place of St Peter's crucifixion. This dignified monument had an important influence on Sir Christopher Wren when he came to design St Paul's Cathedral. The balustrades were a favourite detail in the designs of Oliver Messel.

Brunelleschi (1377–1446) was an important figure of the early Renaissance and his domed churches, including S. Spirito and the Pazzi Chapel in Florence marked a radical departure from medieval ecclesiastical building. Another Florentine architect, Alberti (1404–72), adopted a rigorously academic approach and was the first to set out rules of perspective and proportion. In Rome itself, Bramante was a key figure in establishing the authority of Roman precedents, yet adapted to sixteenth-century Italy. His domed temple, the Tempietto of S. Pietro in Montorio (1502), influenced the design of St Paul's in London over a century and a half later.

The most influential of all Italian Renaissance architects, however, was Andrea Palladio (1508–80). Origi-

nally trained as a mason, Palladio left his home in Vicenza to study the Roman ruins for himself. The scholarly perfectionism of his classical researches is displayed in a series of exquisite villas in the gentle countryside near Vicenza and Venice, notably the Villa Capra (La Rotonda) and the Villa Foscari (La Malcontenta). Begun in 1567, La Rotonda, a square building with a domed central hall and one portico on each of the four faces of the square, was copied all over Europe, but especially in England. Nevertheless, Palladio's most influential work was not a building at all. *The Four Books of Architecture* (*I quattro libri dell'Architettura*) of 1570, in which Palladio set out his precise observations of

The focus of rich carving and decoration, carved chests were among the most significant pieces of Renaissance furniture. The Nerli cassone, with its sumptuous painted panels, is a Florentine example dating from about 1492.

classical design, spread his particular vision of classicism far and wide.

In contrast to the purity of Palladio, the architectural work of Michelangelo (1475–1564), which includes the Medici chapel in S. Lorenzo and the dome of St Peter's, Rome, shows a transition to a freer, more personal interpretation of classical forms. The dramatic intensity of this 'mannerist' approach foreshadows the grandiloquence of the Baroque.

The main tenets of Renaissance classicism were harmony and rationality. The design of buildings, both inside and out, was not the result of a piecemeal organic process but an entire conception deliberately executed. It was also human-centred. The scale and disposition of spaces was intended to create a pleasing sense of beauty that could be appreciated by the human observer standing in the centre of it: this was in stark contrast to the overwhelming sense of awe that was intended to be experienced in Gothic cathedrals.

Renaissance artists and architects had little idea what Roman interiors looked like. But the result of their symmetrical planning and systems of proportion were to set standards by which rooms have subsequently been judged. The interrelated layout of rooms within a building, the human scale and articulation of basic elements within a room and the interdependence of house and landscape date from this time.

The Renaissance idea of a building as a whole entity was extended to decoration and furnishing, which were planned to be appropriate and harmonious. Furniture, although sparse, was monumental and highly architectural, as typified by the huge carved chests or cassoni, ornate tables inlaid with coloured marbles and the new form of the cabinet which was just beginning

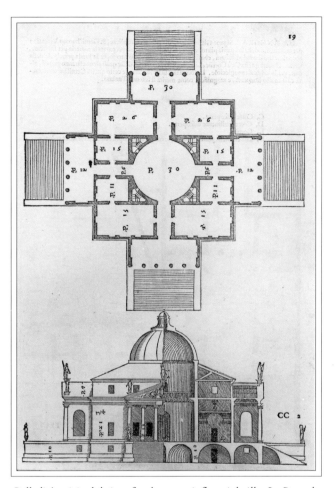

Palladio's original designs for that most influential villa, La Rotonda, Vicenza. The rigorous symmetry of the plan, a square building with a central dome and a portico on each of the four faces of the square, was widely copied in England.

to come in at this time. Walls were sumptuous and rich, covered in tapestry or frescoed in trompe l'oeil scenes. The pursuit of beauty evident in these fine surroundings signalled the emergence of the domestic house as an arena of taste.

The interior of Palladio's Villa Barbaro, Maser, is magnificently enriched by fresco decorations carried out by Veronese. Trompe l'oeil views of ancient ruins alternate with real windows, expressing a desire to link architecture and landscape ever more closely together.

THE SPREAD OF CLASSICISM

Renaissance ideas eventually extended their influence throughout Europe. But progress was uneven, communications poor and traditions in countries far from Rome hard to supplant. The spread of classicism in the centuries after Palladio is not a smooth, unbroken course but a process of adaptation and reaction which can be at times hard to trace.

Travel was difficult and distance played a very real part in the slow pace of development. France was the first place where Renaissance motifs were adopted. Italian craftsmen introduced decorative elements such as scrollwork, masks and garlands to the court of François I, while the Renaissance theorist Serlio was appointed architect to the King in 1540. A few French artists travelled to Rome and pattern books circulated, disseminating classical design ideas. England was even more remote; with the Reformation and the dissolution of the monasteries, links with Italy were virtually severed for a time. Over much of northern Europe, classicism first appeared in the form of decoration, rather than a system of design. Nevertheless, Italian craftsmen were employed by Henry VIII and pattern books were known and reprinted.

Meanwhile, in Italy, the discipline of pure classicism was losing its appeal. In the mid-seventeenth century a new style emerged: the Baroque. In the hands of sculptor-architects such as Bernini and Borromini, measured structural clarity gave way to expressive and lavish effects that merged painting, sculpture, architecture and furnishing in sensuous displays of wealth and status. Italian craftsmen travelled throughout Europe, spreading the style from Portugal to Austria. The extravagant grandeur of the Baroque, particularly its wilder manifestations in Germany and Spain, seems particularly remote from the calmness and order of the Renaissance: it is one of the complexities of design history that the Baroque can either be seen as a manipulation of basically classical ideas, or as their virtual opposite.

At this point France emerged as the centre of European art, a supremacy which remained unchallenged for the next 150 years. The Manufacture des Gobelins, established by Louis XIII to provide furnishings for royal residences, helped to forge a French national style. This design leadership was consolidated during the reign of the Sun King, Louis XIV, whose magnificent Palace of Versailles was pure Baroque not only in its architecture but also in the majesty of its formal gardens. Far more influential, however, was the east front of the Palais du Louvre, designed in 1665 by Charles Perrault (1613–88), a building which dramatically illustrates the power of the Baroque to transform classical elements into something altogether more forceful and theatrical.

England proved largely resistant to Baroque influences, just as it had resisted much of the earlier effects of the Italian Renaissance. The first to bring classical notions of design to England was Inigo Jones (1573–1652), inspired by the pure restrained classicism of Palladio. While described by Pevsner as 'the first English architect in the modern sense', Inigo Jones was a designer in the Renaissance manner and could design anything from a building to a costume. Travels in Italy with his patron the Earl of Arundel provided Inigo Jones with the opportunity to absorb Palladian ideas at first hand, a classical vision which informed

Opposite: The Great Hall in The Queen's House, Greenwich, designed by Inigo Jones in 1616. The first entirely classical building in Britain, its most famous resident was Queen Henrietta Maria, the French princess who married Charles I. She filled the house with sumptuous furniture and commissioned leading artists and sculptors to decorate the interior.

the design of The Queen's House, Greenwich, London in 1616. The plain symmetry of the elevation of this building displays Jones' opposition to the ornamental excesses of the Baroque; its rigorous organization recalls the planning of Palladio's villas. Equally important as a forerunner of English classicism was his 1630 design for Covent Garden, with its use of the Tuscan order taken directly from Vitruvius. The layout of Covent Garden, the first planned London square, was the model for what would become the most characteristic element of Georgian town planning.

No account of the development of classicism and its variations during this period would be complete without Sir Christopher Wren (1632–1723). Like Inigo Jones, Wren never trained as an architect. He was, instead, a scientist, a founder of the Royal Society, an inventor and a professor of astronomy before he became a member of the Royal Commission appointed to rebuild London after the Great Fire of 1666. The restoration of the monarchy in 1660 and the return of the exiled court from Europe had brought a new awareness of French taste to England. Wren, unlike Inigo Jones, took his inspiration from France, by this time the centre of the architectural world. On a visit to Paris he was fired with enthusiasm by the new designs for the Louvre.

St Paul's Cathedral in London, Wren's masterpiece (1675–1710), is accordingly a blend of classicism with the Baroque. The classical dome, described by Pevsner as 'one of the most perfect in the world' was inspired by St Peter's and Bramante's Tempietto, while the facade features paired columns, like those of Perrault's Louvre, and Baroque towers designed after 1700. In this grand design and in the design of the fifty-one

other churches within the City for which Wren was responsible, Renaissance classicism is strongly flavoured by the Baroque fashions of the day.

It was not until the early eighteenth century that great Baroque houses in the manner of European palaces were built in England. Castle Howard (1699–1712) and Blenheim Palace (1705–20) by Sir John Vanbrugh are the best known. The sheer scale and theatricality of these palaces provoked adverse contemporary comment, famously from the poet Alexander Pope who was offended by Blenheim's extravagant splendour. Enumerating the palace's grand apartments he concluded:

'. . . 'tis very fine,
But where d'ye sleep, or where d'ye dine?
I find, by all you have been telling,
That 'tis a house, but not a dwelling.'

His appeal that traditional English common sense and practicality should rule design matters was to be answered by the Palladian architects of the next generation.

The effect of the Baroque on the interior was to establish classical principles of harmony and symmetry. Plans were ordered and symmetrical, with sequences of rooms precisely aligned along a central axis. In great palaces and the houses of the nobility this 'enfilade' magnified the sense of space. But it also enshrined a rigid social etiquette whereby progress from outer chamber to inner apartment marked an upward step in the hierarchy, at the head of which reigned the supreme authority of the monarch.

A lavish use of luxurious materials was integral to these glorious Baroque interiors. Gilding, mirror, marble, murals and exotic woods proclaimed wealth

Opposite: St Paul's Cathedral c.1754 by Antonio Canaletto (1697-1768).
This beloved London landmark, Wren's supreme achievement, was built between
1675 and 1711, replacing the old cathedral destroyed in the Great Fire.

These upholstery designs by Daniel Marot show an early attempt at coordinating fabric treatments.

ionable circles, a coordination of fabrics and styles of treatment which gave a new deliberation to interior design. The chief proponent of this new direction was the French architect Daniel Marot, a Huguenot refugee who initially settled in Holland, but moved to England when his patron William of Orange became William III.

The seventeenth century saw the cabinet evolve from a portable desk or document case to one of the most elaborate and highly prized items of furniture. Resting on its own stand, often with doors enclosing an array of drawers for keeping collections of curios and precious objects, the cabinet became overtly architectural in form; some examples had pedimented tops and columns. It was invariably richly decorated with marquetry and other exotic inlay and the virtuosity of craftsmanship marks the beginning of the transitional stage from upholstery to woodwork as a key element in decoration.

Huguenot craftsmen fleeing the religious persecutions of Louis XIV also found refuge in London, bringing the skills and tastes of the French court to England. Pattern books of interior decoration and design now supplemented those on architecture. French notions of comfort and elegance were avidly followed from Vienna to St Petersburg.

In the form of Baroque, classical ideas had reached all parts of Europe by the beginning of the eighteenth century. The style of kings, princes and powerful church patrons, Baroque had, to some extent, sacrificed the purity of the original classical conception in its dramatic displays of power and wealth. The time was ripe for reaction, and yet another rediscovery of antiquity.

and status. Where these were unobtainable or excessively expensive, impressive imitations in paint and other trompe l'oeil effects were employed.

By the middle of the seventeenth century the classical concept of unity was extended to furniture and furnishings, as well as to decoration and planning. Suites of furniture for specific rooms were designed, with mirror frames, tables, chairs and consoles conceived as an entire ensemble. At the same time, 'en suite' schemes of furnishing became standard in fash-

*The quintessential Baroque piece was the cabinet, and the exacting skills associated with its
construction and decoration meant that cabinetmakers enjoyed an elite status among all the woodworking trades.
This Louis XIV cabinet on a stand features exquisite marquetry, ivory and tortoiseshell inlay.*

CHAPTER TWO

THE GOLDEN AGE OF CLASSICISM

From a modern perspective, the great age of classical design spans the years between the early decades of the eighteenth century and the early decades of the nineteenth. This is the period of Georgian England, Colonial and Federal America, Gustavian Sweden, neo-Classical France, where every sphere of life from the architecture of great houses to the fashioning of everyday household articles was touched by the same vital current of thought.

Looking back from the twentieth century, with all its complexities and uncertainties, it seems a golden age. Taste and refinement, elegance and harmony, poise and grace were the guiding principles not merely of design but of living itself.

The vision of this ordered and enquiring world with its pursuit of perfection and robust practicality has had a powerful effect on our own attitudes to design.

By the eighteenth century, the stage was set for a return to classical principles. In France, critical thought turned away from Baroque extravagances and, with the death of the Sun King in 1715, a new evaluation of classical principles began. In England, where classical ideas had previously achieved only a tentative hold, conversion was rapid and total. Palladianism, pioneered by Lord Burlington and his circle, ushered in a new era of design blending English practicality with the purest classical ideas.

Above: Haga, the country retreat of the Swedish king, Gustaf III, represents the height of neoclassical elegance and refinement.
*Opposite: Chiswick House, the Earl of Burlington's elegant little villa to the west of London, was based on Palladio's Rotonda and was built
to accommodate Burlington's collections; he called it his 'toy' and made constant improvements.*

'COMMODITIE, FIRMNESS AND DELIGHT'

Vitruvian rules, which had guided the great architects of the Renaissance, were introduced to England by Sir Henry Wotton in *The Elements of Architecture* of 1624. Vitruvius' idea, that architecture depends on 'fitness' or being appropriate, struck a particular chord with the English. 'Commoditie, Firmness and Delight', in Wotton's translation, effectively summarizes the entire Georgian approach to design. The notion of usefulness, and the marrying of grace with good sense, is central to eighteenth-century English taste.

Richard Boyle, 3rd Earl of Burlington (1695–1753), was a key figure in establishing classicism in England; it remained, in one form or another, the dominant style for the next century. What Lord Burlington and his circle popularized was a specific classical vision, the pure rationality of Palladio.

It may seem odd, as it did to some contemporary writers, that a style originally conceived in a warm climate, where the light was strong and winters kind, should have found such favour in England. Palladian austerities, dignified in bright sunshine, could be harsh in cold grey weather. But to the Palladian enthusiasts, who added the necessary chimneys and fireplaces to make their classical houses habitable in the English climate, these criticisms were essentially superficial. It was the combination of Palladian sobriety and purity with the inherent flexibility of the classical orders that agreed with the English temperament as no other imported style had previously done. Nor were its effects limited to architecture. The classical orders gave a model for every kind of design, from the fashioning of a wine glass to the trappings of a state bed.

Burlington was introduced to the work of Palladio by the architect, Colen Campbell (1676–1729) whose Wanstead House, built for a banker, was the first large Palladian house in England. Travels in Italy to see the work of the master at first hand led to an important partnership with William Kent who subsequently worked as an architect under Burlington's patronage. The villa Lord Burlington designed for himself at Chiswick (1725) was modelled on Palladio's Rotonda; Chiswick, in turn, influenced the design of scores of other country houses. Other notable early Palladian examples were Holkham Hall, Norfolk (1734) by William Kent, and Mereworth Castle, Kent (1722-5), and Houghton (1722–6) by Colen Campbell.

In England, the leaders of this new movement came, not from court, but from the landed gentry. Henry VIII's break with Rome and the Dissolution of the Monasteries in the sixteenth century had laid the foun-

A robust design for a pier table by William Kent for Houghton, a Palladian house designed by Colen Campbell. Kent's furniture designs were typically monumental and elaborate.

Opposite: Designed by William Kent for Thomas Coke, Earl of Leicester, Holkham Hall in Norfolk was a notable early eighteenth-century country house in the grand Palladian manner. The hall, with its Ionic colonnades, originally housed a collection of sculpture.

dation for the great landed estates through the release of church lands and riches. The reign of Elizabeth I, a period of energetic confidence and prosperity, saw the building of great mansions by families rewarded for services to the Crown.

During the seventeenth century this process was temporarily arrested by bitter political and religious conflicts, culminating in the Civil War and execution of Charles I, which tore English society apart. The Restoration brought French influences to Britain with the return of the exiled court of Charles II; while Dutch styles came to the fore when James II was overthrown and William of Orange came from The Hague to be crowned William III.

By the early eighteenth century and the reign of Queen Anne England had entered a period of stability and prosperity unknown since the golden days of Elizabeth. Victories over the French led to supremacy in trade, and riches flowed into the country. With the coronation of George I in 1714 and the establishment of the new Hanoverian dynasty, the future of the monarchy was assured. The landed gentry with their long-established country seats and new-found political security had both the leisure and the inclination to build a new way of life based on artistic appreciation, enlightened patronage and classical education. And the growth of trade meant there was a rising middle class eager to follow in all matters of taste.

This was the context that provided such fruitful ground for the growth of classical ideas. Through vari-

ous publications, including an edition of Palladio's works sponsored by Lord Burlington and *Vitruvius Britannicus* by Colen Campbell, which comprised engravings of classical building in Britain, the new style gained momentum. Isaac Ware's *The Complete Body of Architecture* was a popular sourcebook. Other guides showed variations on every conceivable feature, from windows to fireplaces, designs which could be copied by other architects, builders or craftsmen. The spread of influence was so rapid that a matter of months was all that it took for an idea to be adopted half-way across the world in the colonies of North America.

Equally important in the dissemination of classical ideas was the fashion for Grand Tours. Continental travel began as an important safety-valve for those wishing to escape Puritan restrictions or the conflicts of the Civil War in the middle of the seventeenth century. By the eighteenth, it had become common practice for young gentlemen to complete their education by making a tour of European capitals, accompanied by tutors, to acquire a first-hand appreciation of monuments and great buildings and to visit collections and libraries. As the century progressed, these cultural forays sometimes were little more than fashionable sprees, exercises in letting off steam rather than pure highmindedness. But it is impossible to underestimate the importance of the Grand Tour in creating a climate of appreciation and discernment necessary for the growth of classicism.

Above: Work in progress on a country house. Informed debate on all matters of 'taste' was a characteristic of Georgian society.
Opposite: 'Charles Towneley in his Library' 1781-1783, by Zoffany. Towneley (far right with his dog, Kam) amassed a great collection
of marbles which was sold after his death to the British Museum. This portrait shows the best of his collection, normally
displayed throughout his house in Westminster, in a somewhat fictitious setting.

The climax of a Grand Tour was a sojourn in Italy, where classical ruins could be visited, studied and drawn. There was opportunity, too, for collecting antique fragments, authentic or reproduction classical sculptures, bronzes, engravings and designs of ruins and Renaissance glories. Young gentlemen, returning home to take their place in the social hierarchy, had often amassed a substantial collection of antiquities as tangible proof of their refined sensibilities. The new classical style offered the means to create temples of art where these treasures could be displayed, visited and admired by all.

This patrician elite was highly educated and critically minded. Throughout the century lively and intense debates raged on all matters of style, architectural detail and ornament. Some of the gentry, like Lord Burlington, were virtuoso amateur architects and designers; others were enlightened patrons. The effect

One of a pair of George III semicircular tea tables, embellished with Grand Tour scenes. The Grand Tour was the climax of a gentleman's classical education.

was to create a progressive and invigorating climate where standards of excellence in all spheres of design could be pursued.

It was not merely in the architecture, decoration and furnishing of great houses that the classical style was expressed. Countless smaller country houses built at this time show the blending of traditional styles and materials with classical elements. Dutch methods of building in brick introduced in the late seventeenth century persisted, but were given a new classical flavour. Neat symmetrical elevations, with rows of sash windows and contrasting stone quoins, crowned with a pediment, were typical features of these quiet, dignified houses which can still be seen in many provincial towns.

A counterpoint to the formality of Palladianism was the new spirit of informality in the landscape, pioneered by William Kent. Landscaped gardens, with their carefully judged natural effects, were a far cry from the rigid symmetries of French formal garden style and betrayed the deep English love of nature. The greatest exponent of this approach was Lancelot 'Capability' Brown (1715–83) who laid out the grounds at Blenheim. Sweeping parkland studded with clumps of trees, lakes and streams crossed by little bridges were the hallmarks of this style.

'Elegant little classical villas set in a park', in the words of John Gloag, show the refined Georgian balance between nature and order. Hogarth was one contemporary commentator who traced, through Vitruvius, the natural forms on which classical ideas were based: nature, he believed, gave 'an infinite choice of elegant hints' for the designer. At the same time, scientific interest in the discoveries of the tele-

scope and microscope provided evidence of natural order in the universe and in microcosm. To the designers of the period, nature and order were not irreconcilable opposites.

TOWN AND SQUARE

What Dan Cruickshank has called 'the orderly flexibility of eighteenth-century architectural classicism' is demonstrated, above all, in the Georgian townhouse. Terraced building was already a well-established tradition in Britain; with the rise of classicism, town planning and development achieved a new coherence and nationality.

Shortage of timber and a keen awareness of the risk of fire had seen brick supersede wood as the principal building material. The introduction of the sliding sash window, which began to replace the old form of the casement at the end of the seventeenth century had an equally radical effect. Glass improved and the sparkling effect of regularly shaped windows gave a new liveliness to ordinary buildings.

The rise of Palladianism coincided with a boom in urban development. Queensberry House, London (1721), designed by a Venetian architect named Leoni, an ardent Palladian, was an early example of how Palladian principles could be adapted in an urban setting. On a more modest scale, the speculative development of London, Bath and other fashionable cities showed classical ideas of proportion and order in practice. Terraces were laid out symmetrically, in neat grids punctuated by squares or circuses. In 1728 John Wood the elder (c.1700–54) created the first English square planned with wholly regular facades after Inigo Jones'

*The ground floor study of Number One, Royal Crescent, Bath. The handsome bureau bookcase and card table indicate
a range of fashionable pursuits and a degree of comfort in the interior.*

Covent Garden. Queen's Square in Bath shows the entire terrace treated as a palace front, with a central portico, a treatment later taken further by Adam in London. Wood's son, John Wood the younger, was the architect of that magnificent sweep of Georgian terrace, the Royal Crescent in Bath.

The pace of expansion meant that not all new houses were executed to the same standard; work could be shoddy and design debased. By the end of the century, building was increasingly controlled by numerous Acts which attempted to rectify bad practices and set standards of design. 'Rate' houses, where fixed categories of house building were established, reinforced the homogenity. The four classes of domestic building, which came into force in 1774, were defined by size, construction and position.

As the century progressed, classicism was incorporated into the pattern of ordinary building with apparent ease. On plain brick townhouse facades, it was the size and position of windows which showed the greatest classical influence.

Following Renaissance precedents, the first floor apartments gradually became the largest and most important. Accordingly, windows at this level were the tallest and most ornamented, with windows higher up becoming progressively smaller and squarer in proportion. The ground floor was often emphasized by a rusticated treatment, again in imitation of Renaissance buildings. No matter how plain or modest the house, the door was always a focus of embellishment, often surmounted by a miniature temple facade.

The humane regularity of these Georgian terraces, with their vistas and green squares, is as important a classical legacy as any great Palladian house or masterpiece by Adam. The individuality of detail and the sympathetic blend of classical rules with traditional forms combine to create a pattern of building which has proved of lasting charm and relevance.

*Opposite: The Royal Crescent, Bath 1767–75, designed by John Wood the younger (1728–81),
a sweeping Ionic parade which set a pattern for British town planning.*

REAPPRAISAL AND REVIVAL

About the middle of the century, yet another revival of classicism occurred. This time it was not Rome or Renaissance Italy that provided the inspiration, but Greece. Rome had been so long regarded as the source of all artistic truth that this new fashion for Greek classicism represented a real upheaval in critical thought.

The Greek Revival was a return to basic principles. It also signalled the beginning of a deliberate use of the past – or Antiquity – as a source of inspiration. This archaeological approach began in 1751 when James Stuart and Nicholas Revett journeyed to Athens, at that time barely accessible to travellers and, like the rest of Greece, then part of the Ottoman Empire. In 1762 Stuart and Revett published *The Antiquities of Athens,* the first in a series of books which provided accurate detailed representations of Greek temples.

The book had a tremendous impact. The simplicity and power of the Doric order, as exemplified by the Parthenon, was revealed to architects for the first time. Equally influential were the etchings of Piranesi (1720–78), a Venetian architect whose published prints of Roman ruins, romantically interpreted, were extremely popular. And, from the 1750s onwards, excavations at Pompeii and Herculaneum provided startling new evidence of the way Romans actually lived, in the form of villas complete with their interior decorations. Although the impact of such discoveries was not felt until later in the century, the trend towards historical accuracy in classical design was well underway by the 1760s.

In France, Abbe Laugier was the first to promote Neoclassical principles. He wrote an influential book urging a return to simple, natural forms (*l'Essai sur l'Architecture,* 1753). It initiated a revolt against the extravagant, highly ornamental Rococo style which had preoccupied French designers in the early decades of the eighteenth century and set a new fashion for austerity. Significant Neoclassical buildings were the Petit Trianon for Madame de Pompadour, built in the gardens of Versailles and designed by Gabriel in 1762, and Soufflot's Pantheon (1755–92). In France, Neo-classicism became associated, not only with the spirit of the Enlightenment but, following the Revolution, with republican sentiments.

The leading architect of the Classical Revival in England was Robert Adam (1728–92), a follower of Piranesi, who established his architectural practice with his brother James in 1758. Adam's light and delicate version of classicism was an entirely new departure and derived from his detailed firsthand studies of classical remains. Palladian followers such as Sir William Chambers, architect of Somerset House, London, and author of the leading eighteenth-century architectural treatise, were scathing in their condemnation of the new style. But Adam's enchanting use of stucco decoration and gracious adaptation of classical motifs won him many commissions, from the remodelling of Syon House and Osterley Park House in Middlesex to the design of numerous London townhouses. His subtle use of colour to enhance spatial effects and unifying use of ornament make him one of the most significant figures in the history of the interior.

Other important architects of the Classical Revival

*The Entrance Hall of Heveningham Hall, Suffolk, 1779 begun by Sir Robert Taylor
and completed by James Wyatt (1747-1813).*

included James Wyatt (1746–1813), responsible for completing Heveningham Hall in Suffolk, and Henry Holland (1745–1806), who remodelled Althorp in Northamptonshire and designed important houses and clubs in London, including Carlton House for the Prince of Wales. At the beginning of the nineteenth century, John Nash (1752–1835) had a highly successful practice, enjoying the royal favour of his patron the Prince of Wales (later George IV). Nash's brilliant exercise in town planning, the Regent Street frontage and Cumberland Terrace, Regent's Park, are models of Neoclassical elegance. But Nash was comfortable designing in other styles, too, as can be seen by the 'Hindu' flavour of Brighton Pavilion.

Sir John Soane (1753–1837) is sometimes regarded as the last Neoclassical English architect. Soane's classicism, however, was idiosyncratic, an almost minimal interpretation of classical form in its use of shallow mouldings. The spatial surprises of his museum of antiquities at Lincoln's Inn Fields (1812–13) reveal a designer of great originality.

By the last quarter of the eighteenth century, Neoclassicism had become the leading international style. In America the Greek style was readily adopted as a means of embodying the democratic principles of the new republic. Colonial houses, not surprisingly, were often very similar to their Georgian counterparts in England; after the War of Independence, French Neoclassical influence was greater. Thomas Jefferson, one of the founding fathers of the republic and the third President, designed the first Neoclassical building in America, the State Capitol in Richmond, Virginia (1789–98), as well as his own house Monticello and much of its furniture. Numerous other public buildings

The Saloon at Heveningham Hall, looking west. Wyatt's classical style closely resembled that of Adam; the interiors at Heveningham are among Wyatt's best work in this manner.

*Above: The Library (built 1792) at 12 Lincoln's Inn Fields, showing
the Soane family at breakfast.
Opposite: The Library at Pitzhanger Manor, Ealing, 1800-2.
Sir John Soane, who remodelled the house, was a master of 'hazard and
surprise' in the interior.*

and great houses made the Greek style synonymous with civic authority and prestige.

In Scandinavia, Neoclassicism was enthusiastically promoted by Gustaf III of Sweden, an internationally-minded monarch who sought to restore Sweden to its former greatness through an enlightened patronage of the arts. A collector of antiquities, Gustaf introduced the Neoclassical style to Sweden following visits to France and Italy. Royal palaces, notably the king's country retreat at Haga, which was modelled on the Petit Trianon, were remodelled or designed in the new classical fashion.

As the eighteenth century drew to a close, much of Europe and North America shared a classical design vocabulary. Classicism, as a system of design, had affected almost every sphere of life. Townhouse and villa, palace and civic building alike were designed, decorated and furnished according to the same set of rules and following the same antique precedents.

The dining room at Monticello, near Charlottesville Virginia 1770-5. Designed by Thomas Jefferson, third President of the United States, the original colonial house was remodelled in a Palladian style.

LIFE IN THE AGE OF REASON

The eighteenth century was an age of complexities. Rapid social change, wars and imperial expansion, the ravages of poverty and disease provided the dark underside of a period we sometimes prefer to see only in terms of its more glorious achievements. The optimism and confidence so characteristic of eighteenth-century life was tempered by more than a fair share of turmoil, discord and uncertainty.

The age of Chippendale, Adam and Hepplewhite was also a time of revolution in France and America, trade wars and land enclosure. Scientific discoveries promised wonderful new insights into the natural world; yet by the end of the century technological advance threatened to change life for ever with the coming of industrialization. Population in Britain grew at a great rate; farm labourers, driven off the land by the effects of the agricultural revolution, were forced to seek work in the cities; many lived and died in the worst conditions of poverty and squalor. Drunkenness was rife, medical knowledge primitive.

Despite these harsh realities (and perhaps, to some extent, because of them), one factor above all distinguishes the eighteenth century from other periods of design. This was 'taste', a positive appreciation and striving for beauty and ease in all aspects of daily life. No other time before or since has ever seen such harmony in design, or such a finely judged balance between beauty and usefulness. From door handle to soup spoon, wine glass to commode, dining chair to glittering reception room, all was elegant, practical and delightful. In the words of historian John Gloag: 'The eye was seldom offended.'

'Shortly After the Marriage' from the series 'Marriage à la Mode' by William Hogarth, 1743. This satire on contemporary morality depicts a fashionable interior of the day. Breakfast is set up on a tripod tea table, while a chimneypiece in the manner of William Kent is loaded with ornaments and statuary.

The preceding pages have shown how classicism came to dominate the world of design. It was a particularly English achievement to translate these ideas of form, proportion and ornament into furniture of the highest quality. Arguably the finest furniture ever made was created by the craftsmen and designers of Georgian England for their discerning clients in elegant townhouses and well-appointed country estates.

The furniture of a period is particularly revealing of the way people lived. The shape of a chair may give us clues about dress and deportment, the carving of a bed may indicate the wealth and position of a household.

'A Gentleman at Breakfast' c.1775, attributed to Henry Walton. The understatement of this eighteenth-century interior looks surprisingly modern. Chairs have checked linen loose covers; the mahogany gateleg table has been set up near the fire and a cheval firescreen can be seen on the extreme right.

While the design and execution of eighteenth-century furniture is ample evidence of exacting standards of the time, its sheer variety reveals the sophisticated range of pursuits of life in the age of reason.

The climate of taste that ruled Georgian England was set by visually educated gentry and wealthy patrons, an attitude that percolated through all upper levels of society. This uniformity, however, did not result in bland standardization but richness and diversity, stimulating craftsmen and designers to achieve new standards in their work.

For many people, life improved and continued to

improve throughout the period. If one compares the furnishings, outside the grandest circles, that were typical in the reign of Queen Anne with those of half a century later, there is a marked increase in comfort. Relatively sparse furnishings gave way to well-appointed rooms with every convenience and refinement.

There was a new awareness of fashion. A host of pattern books and design publications promoted a lively turnover of ideas and craftsmen competed to achieve new heights of sophistication. Neither stagnant nor backward-looking, the eighteenth century welcomed the new. This abiding faith in the future, which gave such impetus to new building and furniture design, is one of the aspects of the age which is hardest to imagine now.

The growing prosperity of the middle classes and relative political stability, at least in England, meant that people were prepared to invest in quality. Furniture was made to last, with the expectation that it would be handed down to succeeding generations. Outside the upper echelons, few people owned their homes. Renting property was usual, a practice which continued during the nineteenth century. In the absence of bricks and mortar to pass on to one's descendants, furniture was seen as a worthwhile investment for the future. But, above all, there was the conviction that beautiful surroundings and fine furniture were necessary for a full enjoyment of life.

The picture of Georgian society which emerges from letters and contemporary accounts is of a lively, competitive world, avid for new fashions and amusements. Eminently civilized in manners and customs, the Georgians nevertheless lacked the inhibitions and sentimentality of their nineteenth-century successors, the

Victorians. Their attitude to life was robust and confident, not hampered by false notions of propriety.

Considering the rigours of travel, there was a surprising degree of mobility. Roads improved during the course of the century and a good turnpike system connected major centres. There were more comfortable, faster vehicles, which meant that women could travel more easily. But off the main post routes, roads were little better than tracks, making for bone-shaking discomfort in summer, impassable in bad weather. Remote country houses and small towns were virtually cut off during the winter.

Yet life was far from static. People moved readily from place to place, travelling to fashionable spas such as Bath and Tunbridge Wells to take the waters or to London to enjoy the attractions of the capital. The custom of paying and receiving calls, and of making prolonged visits to country houses, hastened the spread of new fashions and provided hosts with the excuse to show off their taste and refinement in the display of furnishings and decor. Long before the National Trust came into being, it was the custom for large houses to be open to visitors within 'polite society', which also fostered the spread of ideas from the pace-setting aristocracy to their emulators in the lower gentry.

This increase in travel was matched by greater social mobility. The nobility and gentry mixed freely at large assemblies and balls, at race-meetings and other social gatherings. Strict formality was out of fashion by the middle of the century and this had a great impact on everyday life. Formal state apartments in grand houses gave way to suites of reception rooms for entertaining; by the beginning of the nineteenth century there was a drive to connect house and garden by relocating reception rooms at ground floor level and providing easy access to the grounds.

A separate eating room became more of a standard arrangement. Whereas dining had previously been a movable affair, with folding tables set up when occasion demanded in one of a number of rooms, a distinct dining room with a table left in place was now established. Accordingly, the design of the dining table preoccupied furniture craftsmen during the course of the century. Dining was often a lengthy affair which could take up to five hours; the variety of serving and storage pieces (such as sideboards) shows the great attention paid to the pleasures of the table. Naturally, there was always the risk of over-indulgence. One device was the goutstool, an adjustable footrest to relieve the painful effects of too much rich food and drink.

It was already a long-established English tradition that, after the meal was over, ladies retired from the table and congregated in another room, leaving the men to linger over their port. This social habit was newly reinforced by the fashion for tea drinking, an after-dinner ceremony largely presided over by the women. Dining rooms, accordingly, were 'masculine' enclaves, while drawing rooms (originally withdrawing rooms) were very much in the feminine sphere of

'Tea Chest' from Hepplewhite's 'Guide'.

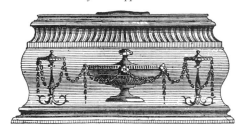

influence. These became much more comfortable, with coordinated furnishings and more upholstery. The old formal arrangement of sitting in a circle gave way in the 1780s to informally arranged conversation groups, so that different activities could be pursued in the same room at the same time.

The craze for tea drinking was more than a passing fad. Its impact on domestic manners – and even furniture design – was considerable. The tea table was a gentle social arena where conversation flowed along with the tea and so-called feminine virtues triumphed. The wide range of furniture associated with tea drinking – tables, caddies, stands and trays – testifies to the importance of this ritual.

Gaming was another popular pursuit. Card tables proliferated, along with a wide range of writing desks and bureaux, in acknowledgement of that other great eighteenth-century obsession, letterwriting. Elaborate dressing tables, with built-in compartments for paint, powder and all the accoutrements of fashion, display the contemporary concern for personal style.

There was a great increase in types of furniture designed to store or display books or collections of fine objects, such as porcelain. Until late in the seventeenth century, even among the aristocracy, few owned many books or paintings; such collections were highly prized and often housed in special rooms or cabinets. But, as the eighteenth century wore on, libraries grew in size and number, and porcelain, paintings, prints and engravings were acquired, not merely by an enlightened elite but throughout fashionable society. Bookcases, cabinets and china cupboards, and carved frames for mirrors and paintings were all designed to meet this new demand.

'The Samels Family' by Johann Eckstein, c.1788 shows a prosperous New England family in their well-appointed drawing room. The mahogany furniture is very similar to English designs of the same period.

In terraced townhouses, space was often limited. A large number of furniture designs from this period ingeniously combined two functions. One example is the press bedstead, a wardrobe containing a fold-down bed. Another is the writing firescreen. A wooden or framed panel on a stand was the standard means of protecting the complexion from the effects of a blaz-ing fire. A writing firescreen consisted of a shallow panel, fitted with compartments for writing materials and with a hinged flap that could be let down and used as a desk, enabling letters to be written by the light and warmth of the fire. In these elegant and practical devices the wit and originality of Georgian designers found full expression.

CHAPTER THREE

A PATTERN OF PERFECTION

The climate of taste in the eighteenth century provided the ideal conditions for fine craftsmanship and design to flourish. Among those who rose to meet this challenge were Chippendale, Hepplewhite and Sheraton, names which today are synonymous with excellence in furniture-making. Then there were architects such as William Kent, Robert Adam and Henry Holland, as well as inspired amateurs such as Thomas Hope, all of whom helped to define the classical furniture tradition.

Eighteenth-century furniture represents a particularly happy balance between elegance and practicality, or 'beauty' and 'use' in the words of contemporary writers. Furniture design also benefited from other fortunate influences which came together in a unique fashion at this time.

Foremost among these was the system of patronage which set high standards of design and execution. The very best furniture was expensive, created for a privileged elite. But furniture for everyday purposes and less exalted clients still aspired to the same standards, even if designs were simplified and decoration less lavish. At the same time, the eighteenth century was the last great period of craftsmanship before the economies of mechanization destroyed the need for such individual talents. And the introduction of a new material, mahogany from the West Indies, provided the perfect medium for craftsmen to display their skills.

As in all areas of design, classicism provided the framework. In form, proportion and ornament, eighteenth-century furniture echoes the same ideas as the great classical houses it was designed to adorn.

Above: A cabinetmaker's office, about 1770. The English furniture trade was centred in London, particularly in and around St Martin's Lane.
Opposite: The Saloon at Kedleston Hall, Derbyshire by Robert Adam. Adam was brought in as a replacement for James Stuart,
whose designs he scorned famously as 'pityfulissimo'.

THE FURNITURE TRADE

The furniture trade of the eighteenth century encompassed a range of craftsmen working in distinct disciplines. Ever since medieval times, joiners had been the most important of these but it was a supremacy that began to be challenged in the late seventeenth century. Joiners, as the term suggests, were essentially concerned with making jointed frames. Much early furniture comprised solid panels, often enriched and adorned with carving, enclosed within a wooden framework.

The beginning of the eighteenth century coincided with the rise of the cabinetmaker. Initially the cabinetmaker had been a specialist in veneering; by the end of the century the term had acquired the more general meaning it has today. Cabinetmakers revolutionized furniture by exploiting new constructional methods, such as dovetailing, to join panels almost seamlessly. The smooth surfaces which resulted could then be decorated with narrow mouldings and two-dimensional finishes such as inlay and marquetry, ideal for the expression of classical themes.

Allied to the rise of the cabinetmaker was the changing role of the upholsterer. The principal function of the upholsterer (or 'upholder') had been to create testers and hangings for beds. With the new emphasis on comfort and seat furniture, the upholsterer found a role covering and padding the seats, backs and arms of chairs and settees, a role which inevitably brought these craftsmen into a closer working relationship with furniture-makers.

In France these trades and crafts were organized in a highly regulated and tightly controlled system. Here the main distinction was between *ébénistes* and *menuisiers*, although there were many supporting crafts including makers of ormulu mounts, crucial in French furnishing. *Ebénistes*, who corresponded to cabinetmakers, specialized in furniture which consisted of a solid carcase covered in veneer and took their name from the fact that much of the veneering on cabinets was done in ebony. *Menuisiers* worked in solid wood and also carried out some carving. Royal workshops, established in the previous century, produced furnishings for royal palaces and coordinated the efforts of the various craftsmen. This function also began to be performed by *marchands merciers*, who traded in exotic goods and materials.

The centre of the less rigidly controlled English furniture trade was London, more particularly St Martin's Lane, which was conveniently near government offices and their rich contracts. The most important cabinetmakers, such as William Vile (*c.*1700-1767) and John Cobb (*c.*1715–1778) who supplied furniture to George III in the 1760s, had their premises here. After 1753 Thomas Chippendale (1718–79) was also based in St Martin's Lane, at 'The Sign of the Chair'.

St Martin's Lane was also the location of the St Martin's Lane Academy, founded by Hogarth in 1735. John Linnell, who later worked with Adam, studied here, probably the first furniture-maker ever to receive design training. With a concentration of artists, craftsmen, architects and tradesmen working in the same area, there was ample opportunity for exchange of views, ideas and skills.

To a large degree the furniture trade remained specialized. Chairmakers made chairs. Turners turned legs for chairs and tables and often produced simple

*Designed by Robert Adam, made by Ince and Mayhew, with gilt mounts by Matthew Boulton,
this 1771 cabinet for Elizabeth, Duchess of Manchester was commissioned as a means of displaying
eleven 'pietre dure' panels by the Florentine artist Baccio Capelli. The gilt-bronze mounts alone cost
£75 11s; Boulton sent them to Ince and Mayhew before gilding to check the fit.*

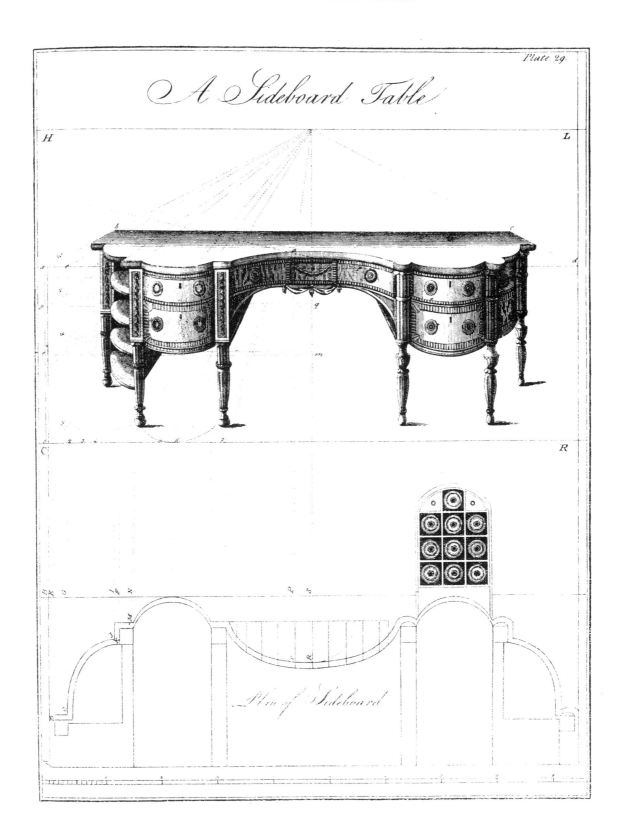

everyday furniture. Carvers, japanners, specialists in marquetry and gilding added their decorative flourishes. But there were also many partnerships of complementary skills: cabinetmakers and upholsterers, framers and mirrormakers, for example, which helped to create an integrated trade.

As the century progressed, successful cabinetmakers were running large workshops, sometimes with showrooms attached. Chippendale was able to offer clients virtually a complete service in interior decoration. An insurance inventory of his premises mid-century lists separate shops for upholstery, japanning and veneering, as well as counting-rooms, living quarters, a showroom and a separate three-storey building filled with cabinetmakers' shops. During this period Chippendale worked closely with the carver Matthias Lock.

One route to success was publication. Published designs advertised the skills of the cabinetmaker, competing for work in a lively and sometimes ruthless market. But the effect of these design books was also to promote the spread of new ideas and fashions, with the consequence that there was always the pressure to come up with something new.

The most important pattern book and one of the most lavish in its presentation was Chippendale's *Director*, published in 1754. *The Gentleman and Cabinet-Maker's Director: Being a large Collection of the Most Elegant and Useful Designs of Household Furniture, in the Most Fashionable Taste*, to give the title in its full glory, included 160 engraved plates displaying designs for a wide range of types of furniture, in contrast to many earlier pattern books which tended to specialize in a single type. With a relatively high price and an impressive subscription list which included five

dukes, the *Director* was a resounding success and influenced many of the design books which followed.

William Ince and John Mayhew's *Universal System of Household Furniture*, published in 1762, owed a debt to the *Director*. In the preface, the authors sounded a note of caution, arguing in favour of restraint and 'Neatness' and against throwing money away in extravagant display.

Other important design books included Hepplewhite's posthumous publication *The Cabinet Maker and Upholsterer's Guide*, 1788, which featured designs in the Neoclassical mode. Sheraton's *Drawing Book*, 1791–4, and *Cabinet Dictionary*, 1803, were equally influential. There were scores of others published throughout the century, ranging from the modest to the extravagant, and the designs they contained were sometimes blatantly copied from other sources or – worse – from competitors. Despite the rather hectic self-promotion, pattern and design books helped to bring new influences to the fore and maintain the intense eighteenth-century interest in style and design.

Above: A commode from Chippendale's 'Director'.
Opposite: A design for a sideboard by Hepplewhite. Many pattern book designs were accompanied by exact dimensions and useful suggestions for construction enabling a skilled craftsman working in the provinces to reproduce standard items.

VARIETY IN THE AGE OF MAHOGANY

The period of fifty years between 1720 and 1770 is famously characterized as the Age of Mahogany. The introduction of mahogany in the 1720s did have a tremendous impact on furniture-making but there were many other woods, both exotic and ordinary, which were also employed. And while wood was the main ingredient of most furniture, a host of other materials from marble, metal and textiles to gilt, paint, cane and gesso had important roles to play.

In the early 1720s, when tax was lifted on colonial woods, the import value of West Indian mahogany was less than three hundred pounds sterling. A mere quarter of a century later, this figure had multiplied a hundred-fold. As a furniture wood, mahogany had much to recommend it. Strong and durable, it was close-grained, good for carving and not prone to shrinkage. Mahogany trunks were big enough in diameter to enable entire table tops to be cut from them. The best mahogany was also attractive enough in its figuring to be used as a veneer. It took a polish well and its pale or ruddy colour mellowed to a beautiful warm brown. Most importantly, mahogany was free from worm.

These advantages meant that mahogany gradually superseded other woods, particularly walnut, as the main material for fine furniture. Comparatively little fine walnut furniture survives because the wood was so susceptible to worm attack but its beautiful figuring meant that it remained in demand for ornamental work well after mahogany was introduced.

At first mahogany was principally used for carved pieces; later cabinetmakers such as Vile and Chippendale perfected the use of mahogany veneer. The light decorated furniture of Adam and the severe Neoclassical designs of Henry Holland were equally well served by this material.

Other prized imports included satinwood from the West Indies, a yellow wood which was so much used in the late eighteenth century that the twenty years between 1770 and 1790 has often been called the Age of Satinwood. Rosewood, with its rich colour and dark streaking, was exceptionally popular during Regency times. Tulipwood, ebony, boxwood and many fruitwoods were used in veneering. If exotic woods were too expensive or hard to come by, native woods might be stained in imitation. Sycamore when stained was known as harewood, a popular veneer at the end of the century.

For the best veneered furniture, the carcase wood was often oak. Otherwise, deal was more usual. Beech was common wood used in chair-making and for upholstered furniture generally; it was often painted and gilded. Elm and yew were two domestic hardwoods often employed in provincial furniture-making, for making Windsor chairs and other traditional designs that altered little over the centuries.

While craftsmen delighted in the colour and natural grain of fine woods, the basic material was just as likely to be a starting point for a range of decorative finishes and embellishments. Veneering was one of the most popular ways of enriching classical furniture in the eighteenth century. Practically speaking, adding a thin layer of expensive exotic wood to a base of cheaper material was economical. The process also enabled woods such as walnut, which could not be cut in very

Opposite: One of the very small number of pieces that can be directly attributed to Chippendale is the magnificent Wilton 'violin' bookcase made around 1763 for the Earl of Pembroke. With a central desk drawer and elegant Rococo carving, the mahogany breakfront bookcase is an outstanding example of Chippendale's genius.

large sections, to be applied in pieces to cover the expanse of a table top or cabinet door. Quarter veneering, where four matched veneers are symmetrically arranged on a table top, was common in the early eighteenth century for this reason.

Veneering was also a way of enhancing pattern and colour without sacrificing the impression of woodiness. Straight cut veneer is taken from lengthwise slices of the trunk but oyster veneer, cut transversely across small branches, and burr, cut from the root or

from warts on the side of the tree, are more overtly patterned and could be pieced together for a more striking effect. Banding, using narrow strips of veneer often in contrasting colours, gave a crisp outline to drawers, tops and panels. Cross banding is laid at right angles to the main surface; straight banding follows the grain of the main veneer. Stringing, applying narrow lines of different woods to the edge of a surface, was very popular in the late eighteenth century.

The form of veneering known as marquetry is al-

This Italian semicircular table of around 1760 features fine marquetry in coloured woods of architectural designs, a virtuoso display of craftsmanship in wood.

together more intricate. Some of the finest examples of classical furniture feature marquetry in virtuoso displays of craftsmanship. The technique, which originated in France, spread to the Low Countries and from there to eighteenth-century English craftsmen, involves creating a design or picture by meticulously piecing together differently grained and coloured veneers. (Where the pattern is geometric, it is known as parquetry.) The result – almost a painting in wood – is a supreme example of how fine furniture-makers mastered the decorative potential of their material.

Painted furniture was popular towards the end of the eighteenth century. Delicate Neoclassical colours – straw, blue-grey and eau de nil – added a touch of lightness to Scandinavian furniture. Lacquered or japanned furniture also enjoyed a vogue due to the persistent fashion for Chinoiserie decoration. Gesso applied to a wooden base could be moulded and then carved into elaborate relief and gilded to make glittering picture frames or marble-topped pier tables. Gilt in general was a luxurious finish for all manner of pieces, from candlestands to console tables.

Gilded bronze or brass were common materials for handles and escutcheons. Inlaid metalwork and galleries for table tops increased in popularity during the Regency period, when furniture was generally more lavish and ornate.

For seat furniture, upholstery materials included velvet, tapestry, damask, watered silk, brocade, wool and leather. The vibrant saturated colours of the early part of the eighteenth century – deep crimson and strong green – gradually gave way to more subdued shades, with striped satin a favourite choice. Floral patterns, pictorial scenes created in embroidery, and stylized damask designs were also popular. Fine upholstery was protected by loose covers, neatly tailored in checked or striped linen.

Chinese chairs from the 'Director'. The fretwork design of these chairbacks reflects the Chinoiserie craze of the mid-eighteenth century.

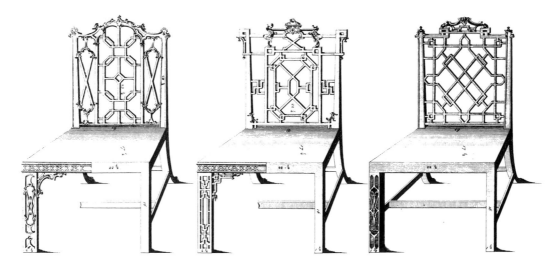

DESIGN AND ORNAMENT FROM KENT TO HOPE

By the end of the eighteenth century English furniture designs were admired and copied all over Europe and throughout America. The key to this English supremacy can be found in the central importance of architecture as an art and the role of architects in creating new forms of furniture in keeping with the classical taste and rationality of their buildings.

The first significant figure in this respect was William Kent (1686–1748), the Palladian designer who enjoyed the patronage of Lord Burlington. When the Palladians emerged as the leaders of taste in the early decades of the eighteenth century and built their splendid country houses and villas, there were no precedents for furnishing in a suitably classical manner. Neither Palladio nor Inigo Jones had indicated how their interiors should be furnished. No furniture survived from Ancient Greece or Rome and, at that time, no one knew what these interiors might have looked like until the excavations at Pompeii and Herculaneum introduced a degree of historical accuracy.

Kent's contribution to the development of classical furniture was more to do with approach than style. In fact, his monumental carved and gilt consoles, pedestals, mirror frames and pier tables have a Baroque extravagance which contrasts with the austerity of their Palladian settings; an example being the interior design and furnishing of Houghton for Sir Robert Walpole. Kent, influenced by Daniel Marot, applied classical ideas of symmetry and proportion in the placing of his ornate furniture; equally important, his furniture was conceived as part of the design of the room as a whole.

The Double Cube Room at Wilton House, Wiltshire, designed by Inigo Jones as the magnificent setting for the Pembroke collection of Van Dyck portraits, contains grand state furniture, heavily carved and gilded, by William Kent.

About twenty years after Palladianism transformed architectural style, classicism began to make its influence felt in other areas of design. This coincided with a rising middle-class prosperity, which meant that there was a new market eager to follow fashionable society in matters of artistic taste. Cabinetmakers addressed themselves to producing a host of new designs, many of which reflected the contemporary obsession with classical architecture.

Upright pieces such as cabinets became overtly architectural in form, with pediments, cornices, pilasters and other elements derived from the facades of temples. Classical styles of ornament featured in the carving of chair backs, chair knees, feet and table legs and in a wide range of other decorative details. Shells, urns, key patterns, swags and garlands, masks, shields, sphinx, griffins and scrolls of acanthus leaves were some of the motifs that imparted the essential classical flavour.

Classicism was not the only influence on furniture design at this period. Unlike France, England proved largely resistant to the extravagant and fanciful excesses of the Rococo style. Nevertheless, certain characteristic Rococo elements, such as gentle serpentine curves, 'C' scrolls, flowers and trailing ribbons, were absorbed into the cabinetmaker's decorative vocabulary. In a similar way Oriental motifs such as latticework show the enduring English fascination for Chinoiserie. Another 'flavour' was the Gothick, a picturesque interpretation of medieval forms. Horace Wal-

Both Chinoiserie and the Rococo style were often expressed in the fanciful carving of mirror or picture frames, as shown by this Chippendale pier glass design.

pole's Gothick flight of fancy, Strawberry Hill, Twickenham, was begun in 1747.

Chippendale became particularly identified with English Rococo. Chairs with backs pierced and carved in sinuous scrolls and leaf forms are particularly characteristic of his work in the middle of the century. At the same time he produced many Chinoiserie designs featuring latticework and imitation bamboo, as well as several other designs with more than a hint of the Gothick. The first edition of the *Director* is no less remarkable for its stylistic variations than the broad range of furniture it contained.

Less than a dozen years later everything had changed. Within a short space of time, Neoclassicism established itself as the dominant style and was to remain so for the rest of the century. The shift in taste was heralded in the third edition of the *Director*, published in 1762, where classical motifs such as key patterns, lion paws and ram's heads began to supplant the exotic decorative influences of Rococo and Chinoiserie. This revolution in design can be largely attributed to Robert Adam, an architect and one of four talented brothers, sons of a Scottish architect.

Adam (1728–92) returned from Rome in 1758 with a classical repertoire drawn from his studies of ancient remains and influenced by his association with Piranesi. From this thorough grounding in classical form and ornament he evolved a personal style which was light, linear, restrained and delicate. Although this new approach attracted controversy and criticism,

Right: London's only surviving great eighteenth-century townhouse, Spencer House, has been meticulously restored to its original grandeur. Lord Spencer was a member of the Society of Dilettanti which sponsored Stuart and Ravett's expedition to Athens 1751-55. On his return, Stuart persuaded Lord Spencer that the state rooms should be a showcase of the new Greek taste. The Painted Room, one of the earliest neoclassical rooms in Europe, contains four sofas and six armchairs specially designed by Stuart for the room; the sofas have curved backs to follow the line of the wall, and feature winged lions in high relief on each side, an idea Stuart derived from an antique marble throne. The suite has been generously loaned by the Victoria and Albert Museum and has now been recovered according to the original design.

especially from staunch Palladians such as Sir William Chambers, the Adam style eventually swept all before it. Chippendale, already a household name, produced what many believe to be his finest furniture of all in the Adam manner.

Adam's early work at Kedleston Hall, Derbyshire, 1759–60, echoed the classical style of the interior decorations designed by James 'Athenian' Stuart several years previously. The furniture Stuart designed for Spencer House, London, in 1759 was also influential, particularly its adaptation of Roman temple features. At Kedleston Adam displayed great originality in his designs for dining room furniture. He is often credited with the invention of the sideboard, a stately composition which, with its flanking urns and pedestals and wine cooler beneath, reflected the ceremonial significance of dining.

Adam furniture tended to be linear rather than curved in Rococo fashion and, as it evolved, lighter and less monumental than early Georgian styles. Table legs were straight and tapering; tops veneered in fine woods or of scagliola. Earlier pieces were often painted white, with gilt ornament; later, after 1780, when painted furniture became more fashionable, he popularized the 'Etruscan' colours, green, black and red.

Much of what Adam designed was 'wall furniture', console and pier tables, mirrors and commodes, intended to be set back against a wall and therefore 'read' as a whole with the wall decoration. Accordingly, Neoclassical motifs and ornament were important features of his designs, since these elements were a means of unifying entire decorative schemes. Shells, honeysuckle (anthemion), palm leaves, scrolls of foliage, festoons of husks and flowers, and medallions depicting classical scenes enriched the simple forms of his furniture. Attention to detail was his hallmark.

Important commissions included the remodelling of Harewood House, Nostell Priory, Yorkshire, and Syon House in Middlesex, 1765. John Linnell (1729–96) and Ince and Mayhew were cabinetmakers who worked

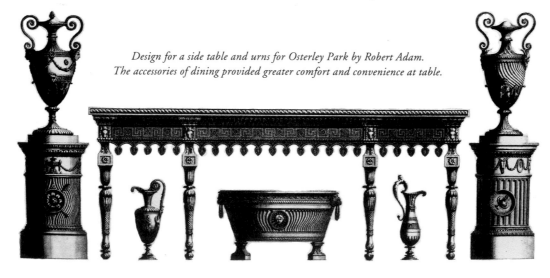

Design for a side table and urns for Osterley Park by Robert Adam. The accessories of dining provided greater comfort and convenience at table.

Chippendale is believed to have made almost all the furniture supplied to Sir Rowland Winn of Nostell Priory, Yorkshire.
The famous Dolls' House is also attributed to Chippendale and richly furnished in marble, silk, chintz, silver, walnut, mahogany, porcelain
and glass, a treasury of craftsmanship and a unique record of life in a great country house. No detail has been overlooked, from
the needlework firescreen in the dressing room to the tiny glass mouse under the kitchen table.

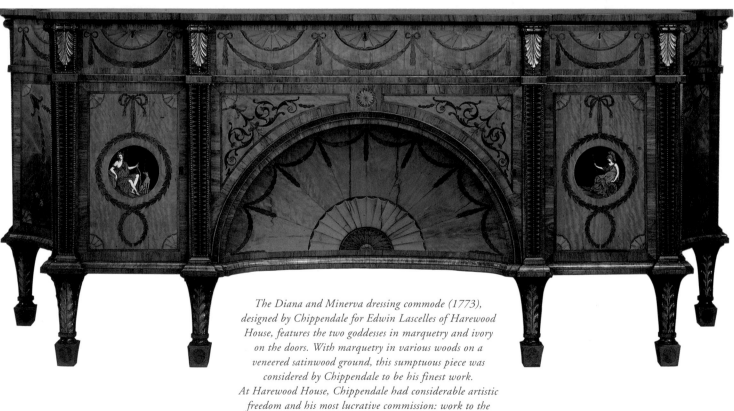

*The Diana and Minerva dressing commode (1773),
designed by Chippendale for Edwin Lascelles of Harewood
House, features the two goddesses in marquetry and ivory
on the doors. With marquetry in various woods on a
veneered satinwood ground, this sumptuous piece was
considered by Chippendale to be his finest work.
At Harewood House, Chippendale had considerable artistic
freedom and his most lucrative commission: work to the
value of over £10,000 was completed by the firm.
The commode cost £86.*

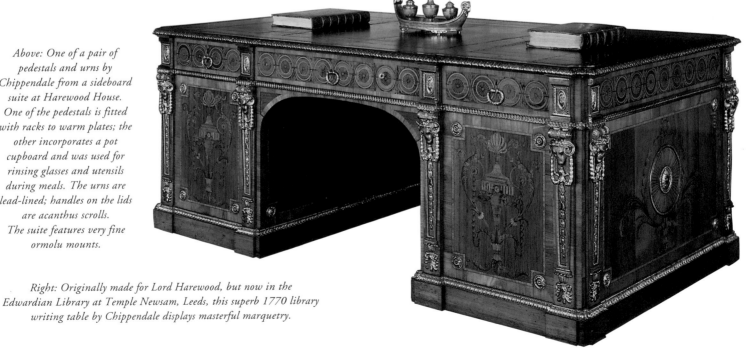

directly to Adam's drawings; Chippendale did not, but produced his own designs in Adam style. A supreme example of Chippendale's Neoclassical work is the magnificent library table at Harewood House (1771), with its harewood, rosewood and satinwood inlay.

Adam's later work, in London at Home House, Portman Square and Apsley House, Piccadilly, and at Osterley Park, Middlesex (1761–80), became progressively more refined and sophisticated. The publication (with his brother) in 1777 of *The Works of Architecture of Robert and James Adam* came at the height of his influence and when what many believe to have been his best work had been completed. Designs produced after this time were often criticized for lack of clarity and excessive ornamentation.

Adam designed for wealthy clients at the highest levels of society, clients who could afford to spend ten times the cost of furnishing a modest house on a single Chippendale table. The range of furniture Adam designed was limited by the fact that it was intended for display in grand surroundings, not for more domestic use. In the last quarter of the eighteenth century many cabinetmakers, some of whom had worked for Adam, brought the new style to the attention of fashionable society. But the person most responsible for translating these classical ideas into furniture for a wider public was George Hepplewhite.

Hepplewhite passed his entire life in obscurity and no furniture survives which can be attributed to him. His considerable fame dates from two years after his death, when his widow Alice published his designs.

Above: One of a pair of pedestals and urns by Chippendale from a sideboard suite at Harewood House. One of the pedestals is fitted with racks to warm plates; the other incorporates a pot cupboard and was used for rinsing glasses and utensils during meals. The urns are lead-lined; handles on the lids are acanthus scrolls. The suite features very fine ormolu mounts.

Right: Originally made for Lord Harewood, but now in the Edwardian Library at Temple Newsam, Leeds, this superb 1770 library writing table by Chippendale displays masterful marquetry.

Above: The Etruscan Room at Osterley Park, designed by Robert Adam, 1775–77.
The classical ornaments were inspired by the decoration on Greek vases and wall paintings at Pompeii.
With chairs set back against the walls in the original arrangement, it is obvious how furniture
and decoration were conceived as a complete scheme, rather than separate elements.
The chairs are painted beech, with cane seats and loose cushions.
Opposite: The Library at Osterley Park. Adam remodelled the sixteenth-century manor house
during the second half of the eighteenth century.

Like Chippendale's *Director*, *The Cabinet-Maker and Upholsterer's Guide* was an immediate success, not least because it was so comprehensive, covering furniture for the bedroom and dressing room as well as the drawing room and dining room. Unlike the *Director*, however, Hepplewhite's *Guide* was stylistically consistent, featuring a graceful, practical version of the Neoclassicism Adam had pioneered. The *Guide* fostered the spread of the Adam style throughout the country.

Hepplewhite's designs, although they were not original, display the Georgian balance of beauty and use-fulness to perfection, admirably succeeding in fulfilling the aims stated in the *Guide*'s preface: 'to unite elegance and utility, and blend the useful with the agreeable . . . and convey a just idea of English taste in furniture for houses'. Sofas and daybeds were comfortable, intended for relaxation; there were designs for bookcases, tallboys, bow-fronted chests of drawers and ingeniously fitted dressing tables to meet a range of furnishing needs. The *Guide* included designs for a new type of sideboard, where table and pedestals were integrated in one space-saving piece. The Hepplewhite secretaire-cabinet harmoniously combined a chest of

Opposite: The Library at Kenwood House, 1767-69, a 'room for receiving company' as well as keeping books, has been described as Robert Adam's finest room. The subtle modulations of the painted decoration and the elegant handling of classical detail are characteristic of his work. Adam remodelled Kenwood in 1764 for Lord Mansfield; his patron, according to Adam, 'gave full scope to my ideas'.
Below: A beautiful 'Bar back Sofa' from Hepplewhite's 'The Cabinet-Maker and Upholsterer's Guide', published by his widow, Alice, after his death.

drawers with a glazed upper cabinet and a fold-down writing surface. At the same time, there were more decorative occasional tables and an elegant series of chair designs, with shield-, oval- and heart-shaped backs. The shield-back chair is particularly associated with Hepplewhite, as is the use of the Prince of Wales feathers as a decorative motif.

Ornament was never lavish or excessive; the designs were intended to be simple enough to be made by ordinary country craftsmen. Yet the use of satinwood and other exotic woods, veneered classical motifs such as festoons, shells, rosettes and medallions, and occa-

sional decorative painting complemented the simplicity of form and gave an air of refinement to the most practical of designs.

The work of Thomas Sheraton (1751–1806) is also known entirely through the publication of his designs. *The Cabinet-Maker and Upholsterer's Drawing Book*, 1791–4, was intended to introduce the latest designs to the rest of the trade. Sheraton, who may never have made any furniture himself, is usually thought to have been the first person to make a living as a furniture designer. He was an evangelical Baptist, and eventually lost his mind and died in poverty.

Pattern book designs disseminated classical ideas. Two designs for ladies' dressing tables and a shield back chair with a central splat in the form of a vase come from Hepplewhite's 'Guide'.
Opposite: Sheraton's elegantly attenuated designs had a wide influence. The parlour chair, tripod firescreen and pier table come from his 'Drawing Book', 1791-4.

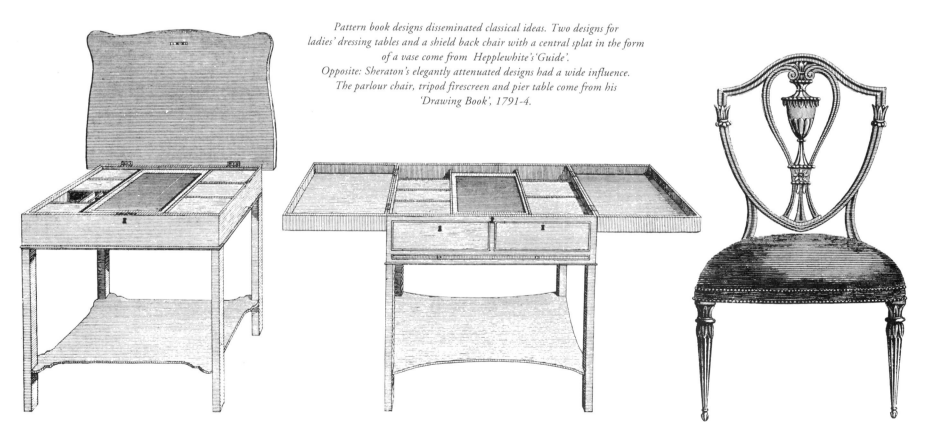

Bridging two main phases of classicism, Sheraton's style was simple in form, even severe, the height of restraint. Legs were thin, reeded and tapering with splayed claw feet; the overall impression of his furniture was of delicacy and elegance. Decoration and ornament displayed a positive appreciation of the beauty of wood, with contrasting veneers, fine stringing and geometric patterns. Classical motifs such as urns, swags and vases were finely executed.

French influences are apparent in his designs, particularly in the reintroduction of serpentine curves in the lines of tables. Floral and ribbon decoration were also French in inspiration. In general, many of Sheraton's designs are smaller, in keeping with the new mood of informality in room arrangement which demanded that furniture be easily moved from place to place as need arose. Cabinet pieces were lower, enabling pictures to be hung in the free wall space. There was the first appearance of the 'Grecian couch', one of the most characteristic of all Regency pieces, while the typical Sheraton chair had a square back and thin turned legs.

Sheraton published designs by Henry Holland (1745–1806), who had recently carried out work for

These scenes of fashionable Regency life, as depicted in 'Designs of Modern Costume' by Henry Moses, 1812 (for Thomas Hope), show how the antiquarian taste permeated every aspect of design, from dress to furniture.

the Prince of Wales at Carlton House. The Prince of Wales (later George IV) was one of the greatest patrons of the arts in English history and it is entirely fitting that the last period of classical design takes its name from the years of the Prince's regency (1811–20), although 'Regency' is a modern term, not a contemporary distinction. The furnishing and rebuilding of Carlton House as the official residence of the Prince Regent provided the impetus for the new classical approach. Both Holland and the Prince were ardent francophiles and some of the furniture for Carlton House was commissioned from craftsmen who supplied pieces to the court of Louis XVI.

By the turn of the century archaeological discoveries at Pompeii and Herculaneum had provided a wealth of new information about the ancient world. It was now possible to distinguish clearly between Greek and Roman forms of classicism; artefacts uncovered at the excavations furnished new sources of decorative detail and ornament. The effect was to create a taste for historical accuracy in design.

Holland, architect to the Whig aristocracy as well as to the Prince, was a pioneer in this respect. Although

he never made the Grand Tour himself, he sent the architect Charles Heathcote Tatham, brother of the cabinetmaker who supplied furniture for Carlton House, to Italy for three years to study classical ornament. Holland's designs reveal a new severity, refinement and a precision of detail in keeping with the emerging Regency style.

Perhaps the most influential figure of this last phase of classical design was not an architect, designer or cabinetmaker but a wealthy son of a banking family, Thomas Hope (1768–1831). Hope, a self-styled 'Modern Greek', was a connoisseur of the ancient world. At the age of eighteen he had made one of the most extensive Grand Tours of the time, spending eight years travelling throughout the Eastern Mediterranean, from Greece and Turkey to Egypt and Syria.

On his return Hope began designing furniture to provide suitable settings for his collections of antique sculpture and vases, on display in his London house in Duchess Street. The publication of these designs in *Household Furniture and Interior Decoration*, 1807,

Opposite: Commode designed by Henry Holland for Southill Park, Bedfordshire, the home of the Whitbread family. Rebuilt by Holland in the 1790s, Southill was one of Holland's most important commissions and remains a significant example of the late classical style. The commode, still in the position for which it was designed, is in rosewood banded with ebonised borders which set off gilt mouldings and ormolu mounts.

was extremely influential in establishing the fashion for the archaeological approach in general and Grecian taste in particular; Hope's Grecian chairs, with their sabre legs, round knees and curved backs are direct

A mahogany circular table with ebony inlay by Thomas Hope. Hope, who called himself a 'Modern Greek' was hugely influential in popularizing Grecian taste, but took his ideas from the whole of the ancient world.

copies of the Greek klismos featured in the painted decoration on vases. Cross-framed stools also displayed their classical antecedents.

Hope drew equally on ancient Egypt and the Far East as sources of inspiration. Sphinxes and hieroglyphics were decorative features of his designs in the Egyptian taste. Although Hope's contribution to classical furniture design was to simplify forms and 'purify' taste, his scholarship was undeniably eclectic. Taking ideas from the whole of the ancient world, France and the Far East resulted in a mingling of influences that foreshadowed the stylistic muddle of Victorian design. Hope's designs were popularized in the pattern books of George Smith, a leading cabinetmaker of the period, who introduced the circlar dining table. Another key figure of the Regency was George Bullock, whose designs appeared in the influential Ackermann's *Repository of Arts*.

At its best, Regency furniture is a byword for elegance and grace. The beautiful curves of sofas and couches with their scrolled ends epitomise the clarity of the Greek style. Light writing tables and sofa tables, a new version of the Pembroke table, were equally refined. Dining tables were supported on central pedestals. The sweeping lines of the Trafalgar chair, commemorating Nelson's famous victory in its nautical detail, married classical form to popular sentiment.

Animal heads and lion paw feet were added to the established classical vocabulary of key patterns, honeysuckle and acanthus scrolls. Double lotus leaf ornament, sabre legs and lyre-shaped supports were prevalent in Hope's designs. The star was another

*George Smith was a leading cabinetmaker of the Regency period. This pair of simulated bronze and parcel-gilt 'bergères' are
after a Smith design. The striking contrast of black and gold, scrolled back, animal heads and feet and star motifs are all characteristic
of this period. Smith based many of his designs on those by Hope and Percier and Fontaine.*

important Regency motif. There was a delight in exotic woods such as yellow striped calamander and a fashion for rosewood set off with ebony, a colour combination which echoes Pompeiian red and black decoration. Wood painted to look like marble, bamboo or stained and grained to simulate the finish of a more expensive material was also common. Much of Hope's furniture was executed in mahogany set off with metal inlay; from 1812 a revival of brass inlay or

boullework, popularized by the Prince Regent's collection of French furniture, added richness and glitter.

The Regency period saw the final flourishing of the classical spirit as a unifying force in furniture design. Despite the wide range of influences, both classical and contemporary, the fundamentals of design remained true to classical notions of form and proportion. This exquisite sense of poise was soon lost with the coming of industrialization.

THE FRENCH INFLUENCE

France was the unquestioned leader of the fashionable world throughout much of the eighteenth century. Under royal patronage, craftsmen developed their skills to the height of perfection, and were rewarded accordingly. A taste for luxury and extravagant display in court circles and among the aristocracy was satisfied by ever-increasing inventiveness and finesse. 'No fashion is meant to last longer than a lover', quipped Horace Walpole in 1766, remarking on the rapid turnover of French styles. The demand for fine furniture was so great that craftsmen were drawn from other parts of Europe, particularly from Germany, to work in Paris.

French influence, although powerful, was also uneven. Wars interrupted the smooth flow of ideas, materials and goods. The cataclysm of the Revolution signalled the end of a way of life and dispersed royal collections. And France lacked the type of design leadership provided in England by architects such as Kent, Adam and Holland.

Opposite: Napoleon's bedroom in the Grand Trianon at Versailles has been restored in Empire style, with chamois, lilac and silver hangings in a pattern designed by Empress Josephine. The Grand Trianon, formerly the residence of Madame de Maintenon and Madame de Pompadour, was Napoleon's favourite country retreat.

A mechanical table made for Marie-Antoinette, c.1778, by Jean-Henri Riesener and the mechanic Mercklein. The table could be put to different uses – its ingenious mechanism allowed it to be used for eating, as a dressing table or as a writing table in two positions – and the Queen was said to have kept it constantly by her. It features fine marquetry in satinwood, lavish decoration and secret compartments.

The influx of Huguenot craftsmen at the end of the seventeenth century brought French design ideas and skills to Britain and to the other Protestant countries where they had sought refuge. The French fashion for Rococo decoration was introduced this way and through publications such as the designs of Meissonier (c.1693–1750). Although English Rococo never approached the frivolous extremes of its French counterpart, it had important effects on furniture design.

The flowing curves, asymmetries and fantastical motifs of the Rococo were fundamentally contrary to the spirit of classicism. This did not prevent English craftsmen and designers such as Chippendale and

This satinwood table was designed by the Palladian architect Sir William Chambers and made by Georg Haupt, the leading Swedish cabinetmaker of the neoclassical style, in 1769. The top is inlaid with specimen marbles.

Daybeds with scrolled ends and extravagant beds swathed in drapery were characteristic of the period.

In the exchange of classical influences throughout the eighteenth century, France retained its reputation for furniture of the highest luxury and most superb craftsmanship. As a symbol of taste and status, furniture in the Louis XVI style was eagerly sought all over Europe, from the court of Catherine the Great in Russia, to Spain, Portugal, Germany and Scandinavia. After the Revolution the market was flooded with fine examples from royal and aristocratic collections, a quantity of which was bought for private collections in England. Despite a sometimes uneasy relationship between the two countries, the English gentry, following the Prince Regent's lead, often patronized French craftsmen and *marchands merciers*.

Yet English influences abroad were equally strong. Anglomania was at its height in France in the 1780s and between 1815 and 1825; the pattern books of Chippendale, Hepplewhite and Sheraton had as wide a dissemination as the court furniture of Louis XVI. English goods also found their way to Italy, Germany, Spain, Portugal and Scandinavia, but especially to Holland, where fears that the native furniture industry would be swamped led to a ban on imports from 1771.

As the century progressed Neoclassicism had become a truly international movement. Craftsmen working in their native countries rivalled the expertise of the French and English. Examples include Georg Haupt (1741–84), the leading Swedish classical maker, and Guiseppe Maggiolini (1738–1814), who worked in Milan and was famous for his commodes and for superb pictorial marquetry. He is said to have used eighty-five different woods in the year 1795 alone.

CLASSICAL DESIGN
IN AMERICA

It is not surprising that eighteenth-century furniture produced in North America should follow closely the styles initiated in England. To begin with, local craftsmen drew heavily on the methods and designs of their native country. Even after the colonies became independent in 1776, links with British design remained strong. A distinct American classicism arrived rather later and was more consciously influenced by France in its attempt to express the ideals of the new republic.

There was an understandable time lag in spread of new fashions and ideas. From about 1725 to 1760, American furniture echoed the styles current in the reign of Queen Anne in its S-curves and cabriole legs. As in England, mahogany and walnut were favoured woods, but supplemented by native species such as maple, cedar and cherrywood, while pine, ash, maple and chestnut were carcase materials. Relatively few pieces were veneered, since solid construction better withstood the rigours of the climate.

Although furniture continued to be imported from Europe, especially Britain, the high expense stimulated the growth of a native industry. The main centres of furniture-making at this time were Boston, Newport and Philadelphia and each soon evolved individual characteristics. Boston, a thriving and successful port, had 150 furniture-makers by the time of the Revolu-

A Philadelphia Chippendale-style high boy, mahogany and mahogany veneer, made in the late eighteenth century, with a 'Pompadour' finial bust. Rich carving is characteristic of the Philadelphia Chippendale school; noted makers include Savery, Randolph, Tufft and Trotter.

This reconstruction of a Baltimore drawing room includes a cylinder desk and bookcase based on Hepplewhite and Sheraton designs and probably made in Maryland. The chairs are fine examples of Martha Washington armchairs; and the side chair is a Maryland version of a Sheraton design.

tion. Block-front furniture was especially associated with New England; block fronts of case furniture were composed of three flattened curves, the central concave, the outer convex. Boston was also noted for bombe-shaped pieces, while Newport was particularly associated with carved shell ornament on dressing tables, chair crests and bookcases. Philadelphia, the largest and richest of the three cities, was the home of many craftsmen who had originally trained in London. William Savery (1721–88) was one of the best-known Philadelphia cabinetmakers. Here 'architectural' pieces in the Palladian manner were made. Highboys (tallboys) and chests-on-chests had broken-arch pediments.

Chippendale's *Director* had a tremendous impact on the development of American furniture design, intro-ducing a Rococo lightness to carved ornament. In Philadelphia, Thomas Affleck (1740–95) worked in the Chippendale style. New forms were introduced, including the Pembroke table.

After the War of Independence came the Federal period (1785–1810) which took its name from the ruling political party. Federal style represented a deliberate break with the past, although this did not mean initially that English design was any less influential. Hepplewhite and Sheraton provided the inspiration for many cabinetmakers, including the Seymours, John and his son Thomas, who emigrated from Scotland and became established in Boston after 1794.

The design books of Hepplewhite and Sheraton prompted the use of veneers instead of carving to enrich and decorate, although carving was still import-

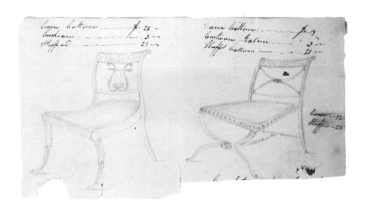

Duncan Phyfe sketches for a lyre-back chair. Phyfe, a leading maker in New York in the early nineteenth century, popularized a personal interpretation of Grecian design elements.

ant in centres such as Salem where the great carver Samuel McIntire (1757–1811) worked. The use of exotic woods became more common, including satinwood, ebony, and bird's eye maple, alongside native woods and mahogany. The eagle, symbol of American statehood, was a common motif.

American classicism was a blend of English influences, assimilated via the works of Adam, Hope, Sheraton and Hepplewhite, with French Neoclassical and Empire styles. The design elements were predominantly Greek, in keeping with the affinity the founders of the new republic felt for ancient democratic ideals. New York was an important new centre. Duncan Phyfe (1768–1854) was among the first to popularize Grecian elements in a personal style of his own, including the klismos chair form, lyre-shaped backs, cross-lattice backs and reeded legs, as well as feather and swag motifs. Charles-Honore Lannuier (1779–1819), born and trained in Paris, was a leading figure in bringing French Empire style to the fore and one of

a number of French craftsmen who took their skills to the new country.

Philadelphia, the capital until 1800, retained its pre-eminence for a time. Bookcases and fall-front secretaires were decorated with large ovals of contrasting veneers. Chairs were made in the Hepplewhite and Sheraton manners. Towards the end of the century, Baltimore became another centre of distinction. John Shaw (1745–1829) worked at nearby Annapolis following Hepplewhite's style. Gold and black painted glass panels (*verre églomisé*) was a speciality of Baltimore, as was marquetry.

Tambour desk by John Seymour and Son, 1794-1804, in mahogany. From the Federal period, this design shows the influence of Sheraton in its spare, elegant neoclassical lines.

A magnificent mahogany desk and bookcase in the Chippendale style, made in Rhode Island and attributed to the Newport Quaker John Goddard (1723–1785). The carved shell motif and block front is characteristic.

*Made for Margaret Oliver of Baltimore in 1811,
this mahogany, satinwood and 'verre églomisé'
bookcase desk is modelled on the 'Sister's Cylinder
Bookcase', plate 38 in Sheraton's Cabinet
Directory of 1803.*

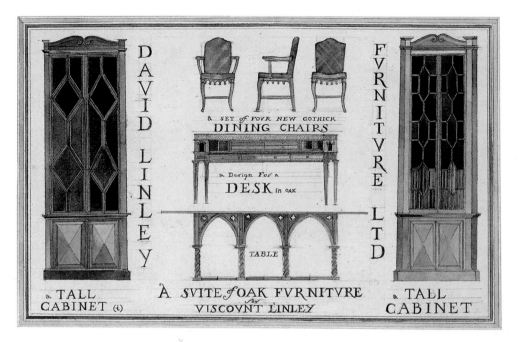

DAVID LINLEY

FVRNITVRE LTD

a SET of FOVR NEW GOTHICK
DINING CHAIRS

a Design For a
DESK in OAK

TABLE

A SVITE of OAK FVRNITVRE
for
VISCOVNT LINLEY

a TALL
CABINET (4)

a TALL
CABINET

A DIRECTORY OF FURNITURE

All furniture is a product of its time. The classical furniture of the eighteenth century is a vivid reminder of that age and its celebration of taste and elegance. At the same time, the proliferation of new types of furniture to serve a range of new pursuits reveals a society moving forward with confidence and curiosity.

Furniture also enjoys a fundamental connection with human life which is not necessarily present to such a degree in other artistic spheres. People move, sit, lie, or stand in certain ways and these basic traits must always be accommodated for furniture to be both comfortable and useful. The human

dimension of furniture design is often acknowledged in the terms we use to describe different parts of a piece: 'knee', 'leg', 'foot', 'elbow', 'arm', 'back' and so on.

Classical furniture is often prized for the sheer craftsmanship it displays, for virtuoso displays of marquetry, intricate carving or delicate inlay. But it is equally valuable for maintaining a constant awareness of basic principles of practicality. The best examples in this tradition do not allow us to forget that they were made for the convenience of those who were to use them.

CHAIRS

Chairs, almost more than any other type of furniture, reveal social preoccupations. During the course of the eighteenth century, chairs became simpler and more elegant, while all seat furniture showed a new concern for comfort.

The 'back stool' or chair without arms was a relatively late form of seating, appearing in the seventeenth century. Before this time, stools, settles and benches made do for ordinary purposes and chairs were specifically armchairs. The introduction of mahogany in the eighteenth century meant that chairs could be made much stronger than before, but it also provided a medium for expressing new design influences since it could easily be carved and pierced in a variety of ways.

The variations of style in eighteenth-century single chairs are often concentrated on the shape of the back and the design of the back splat. The back splat was particularly important in determining the style of Chippendale chairs. Hepplewhite was associated with the shield back, but also designed oval-, heart- and lyre-shaped backs; Sheraton's chairs were more upright and rectilinear. Regency chairs were often made with swept back top rails.

Chair legs in the early part of the century were largely cabriole legs, gently curving and often ending in a ball and claw foot. The form of the cabriole leg, echoing the curves of Rococo design, nevertheless had a more ancient origin, referring back to the animal legs found on Greek and Roman furniture; while the ball and claw foot is thought to have been taken from the Chinese and supposedly represents a three-clawed

The chair presents the most challenging design task; it must be comfortable, tailored to the human form, and despite the great number of joints, remain strong enough to withstand tipping up or leaning back. The simple upholstered chair (above) is from the Linley Classic manufactured range; our hall chairs (right) are in solid sycamore, with Swiss pear and Vavona burr backs, Macassar ebony inlaid around the seat rail and tapered legs.

dragon holding a pearl. As the influence of classical design increased, chair legs became straight and tapering, reaching a fine degree of elegance with Sheraton. The sweeping line of the sabre leg on Regency chairs was a version of the same feature on the Greek klismos. Fluted or reeded legs also date from the end of the period.

Such chairs were generally made in even-numbered sets, perhaps including a pair of elbow chairs, and reflect the new emphasis on dining. Seats were upholstered in matching fabric. Side chairs, designed to

stand against a wall, were upholstered en suite with the rest of the room's furnishings and might be both larger and more ornate, for display rather than sitting on. From this time there was a conscious attempt to unify furniture with decoration and a set of seat furniture, in matching material, might consist of chairs, couches and stools. The backs were often left plain or uncovered, since they would not generally be on view. Hall chairs, descendants of the Renaissance sgabello, had solid backs and seats and were often painted or elaborately carved with coats of arms.

Both the elaborate dress of the times and social customs called for an upright posture but concessions were increasingly made to comfort. Chair backs were gently inclined to support the spine, seats were wide and arms set back to allow for voluminous skirts and coats. France led the way in creating new types of upholstered chair, including the *bergère* with its padded sides and various forms of fauteuil or armchair

with padded elbows. In England the wing chair, which first appeared in the late seventeenth century, remained popular. Its enclosing shape, with padded back, seat, arms and 'wings', provided effective protection against draughts.

Less familiar are a number of other types of chair, many of which were designed to fulfil a particular function. The corner chair had a square seat, angled so that there was a single cabriole leg in front, enabling gentlemen to sit astride, a comfortable position for writing at a desk. The conversation chair had a padded top rail; gentlemen, sitting back to front, could lounge informally leaning on the top rail, while at the same time keeping coat skirts uncrumpled. Reading chairs were also for sitting backwards and had a little adjustable desk fixed to the back and candle holders attached to the arms.

Classical chair backs display variations in style, from the neoclassical elegance of Sheraton (far left), to the characteristic shield shape of Hepplewhite (centre) and the familiar scrolled carving of Chippendale (below).

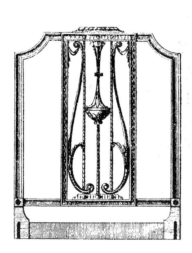

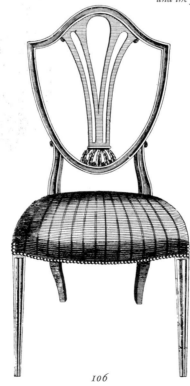

Left: Variations on a theme by Hepplewhite. The Gothic detail of the chair back (near left) reflects a contemporary fashion.
Below left: Sheraton drawing room chairs, with their comfortably padded seats, show a French influence.

Below: Among the best known of all Chippendale chair designs, 'ribband back' chairs display the designer's mastery of Rococo elements. 'If I may speak without vanity, they are the best I have ever seen,' wrote Chippendale.

Left: This comfortable 'bergère' was made by Chippendale for David Garrick around 1750.
Right: Also by Chippendale, working to a design by Robert Adam, the carved and gilded chair was made for Sir Laurence Dundas at Arlington Street in 1765. This commission is the only occasion in which Chippendale is known to have made one of Adam's designs; it also represents his first known neoclassical work.

Below: One of a pair, this fine Hepplewhite mahogany shield back armchair features carved Prince of Wales feathers forming the entire back splat and was made in England around 1780.

Left: Eighteenth-century over-indulgence could be relieved with the aid of the 'gout stool' which allowed the painful foot to be elevated. This example is a Hepplewhite design.
Right: Also by Hepplewhite, a high-backed wing chair shielded the occupant from chilly draughts. This design from 1788 is described as an 'easy' chair or 'saddle check' chair.
Far right: An ornate design for a 'French chair' by Chippendale. Mahogany was the ideal material for intricate carving; Chippendale states that 'a skilful workman may also design the carving, without any prejudice to the design'.

Right: A pair of Adam oval-backed gilt carver chairs (c.1780) display the sober elegance of neoclassicism.

Below: Like much Regency furniture, this beech armchair (c.1800) is painted and gilded and has a cane seat.

Below right: The delicacy of Regency chair design is evident in these examples of bedroom chairs from a contemporary London magazine, 'Ackermann's Repository', which reproduced designs based closely on those by Percier and Fontaine.

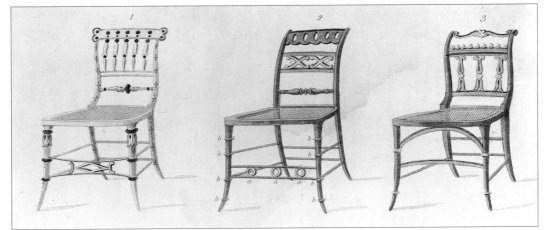

OTHER SEAT FURNITURE

The settee, derived from the settle, was another relatively new form of seating. In the early eighteenth century, settees often took the form of multiple chairs, double or triple backed. Fully upholstered settees, also known as sofas, came later on. These upright pieces, with upholstered seats, backs and sides, often had carved or gilt wooden frames; some were particularly rich and extravagant. The quaintly termed love seat was a form of sofa for two people. Following French influence, the backs of such pieces were gently curved in a manner sympathetic to lines of panelling: such pieces were initially intended to be placed with their backs against the wall.

A greater degree of comfort and informality was provided by deeply upholstered day beds and couches for reclining and lounging. Many of these originated in France and there were a variety of forms, often intended for use in a boudoir. The duchesse brisée was a rounded-back chaise longue usually made in two or three parts so that each section could be used separately for seating.

Later in the century and into the Regency period, the Neoclassical influence transformed the shape of sofas and couches. The Grecian couch, severe and elegantly classical, as can be seen in David's famous portrait of Madame Recamier, was an early version; later Empire and Regency chaises longues had scrolled arms and sinuous backs. Sofas, too, often had high arms scrolled outwards; by the turn of the century such pieces were no longer exclusively placed against a wall, but began to be pulled forward into the room, perhaps in a pair flanking the fire, in the new informal fashion.

A sofa, with pretty scrolls carved in walnut, made by David Linley Furniture for the Cropsey Museum, Hastings-on-Hudson, New York.

Above: Original drawing by Robert Adam of a 'sopha', one of a suite of four, made by Chippendale for Sir Lawrence Dundas to Adam's design. Below: A 'duchesse' was a daybed made in two or three parts so that each one could be used separately; this design is by Hepplewhite.

Above: The Chippendale mahogany carved hall settee (c.1770) shows a reworking of a traditional form.
Below: Festooned with swags of drapery and elegantly curved, this 1793 design for a chaise longue was published in Sheraton's 'Drawing Book'. Such pieces were intended for daytime repose in boudoir or bedroom.
Below right: Exquisitely understated, this Hepplewhite sofa design is timeless in its simplicity and refinement, the curves of arms and back discreetly emphasized by close nailing.

The French influence is evident in this design for a 'burjair' ('bergère') by Ince and Mayhew. The inclined back, padded arms and thick seat cushion reflect a new awareness of comfort.

The gentle scrolling curves of this window stool, with its sparing use of classical detail, would have made a perfect complement to an elegant Georgian window bay. Window seats were very popular at the end of the eighteenth century; this design is by Hepplewhite.

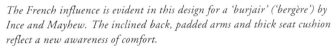

A daybed or 'veilleuse' from around 1750 by Tilliard. The style of the carving on such pieces was often intended to complement wall panelling and mouldings.

By the Regency period, the daybed or chaise longue had acquired a more Grecian flavour with scrolled arms and classically inspired decoration. This rosewood example features brass inlay which became popular in England after 1810.

Settees in the form of multiple chairs were a popular pattern. This quadruple chairback settee is part of a suite of Regency seat furniture, painted in simulation of rosewood and part gilded.

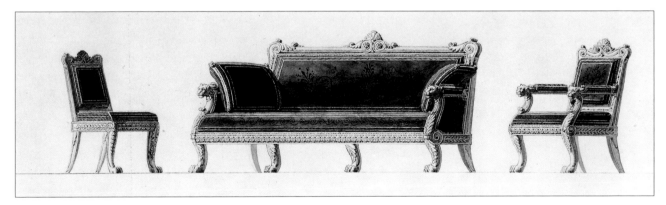

Sofa and chairs designed by Sir Jeffrey Wyatville (1766-1840), the nephew of the architect James Wyatt, for Windsor Castle.

Commissioned by George IV, Wyatville supervised the extensive restorations carried out at Windsor Castle during the early

decades of the nineteenth century. Wyatville, like his uncle, is best known for his work in the 'Gothick' manner.

TABLES

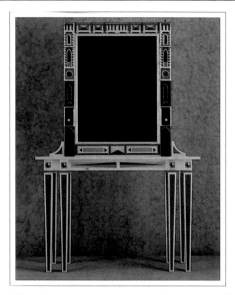

Console table and mirror in sycamore, with Swiss pear and harewood inlays, made by David Linley Furniture. The mirror features marquetry designs inspired by Venetian architectural detail.

The eighteenth century saw a proliferation of table types, and the variety of terms gives a vivid picture of the range of interests and pursuits of the time. There were tables for gaming and playing cards, for writing, dressing and drinking tea, for the bedside, for embroidery and needlework, as well as a range of occasional and side tables. (The dining table, a form which saw considerable development during the period, is treated under 'Dining furniture'; 'Writing furniture' is also covered in a separate section.)

Small tables for specialized use were a French introduction but had universal popularity. Light enough to be easily moved from place to place as need arose, they were the focus of considerable refinement in design and decoration. A new range of furniture was associated with the tea ritual. The tea table, a form dating from about 1720, often had a galleried top which provided a degree of protection for the china tea service. Tilting tripod tables were in wide use as occasional tables. The three-legged base made the table particularly stable on uneven floors and the top could be swung up to a vertical position so that the table could be neatly stowed against the wall when not in use. Urn or kettle stands were fitted with a sliding platform for the teapot or tea bowl; some were low enough to be stored under the tea table.

The Pembroke table, a small occasional drop-leaf table with square, round or oval hinged flaps, originated in the middle of the century; according to Sheraton they are named after 'that lady who first gave orders for one of them', the Countess of Pembroke. The Pembroke table proved to be an indispensable design and was especially popular in America. Its successor, the sofa table, appeared around the turn of the century. Long and narrow, with flaps at each end, it stayed in front of the sofa and catered for a range of uses. Nests of small occasional tables (quartetto tables if there were four; trio if there were three) were fashionable from the late eighteenth century on, and reflected both the relaxing of rigid drawing room formalities and the need to save space. The drum table, for use in drawing rooms, libraries or halls, had a round rotating top on a pedestal base. Drawers fitted around the circumference could be used for storing documents. Towards the end of the period, the 'centre' table began to emerge, a circular table left in the middle of the room to accommodate a range of activities. Work tables, fitted with compartments for sewing

materials, date from the middle of the century. Prettily decorated, sometimes with marquetry, such pieces often incorporated a silk bag for keeping silks and pieces of work. Dressing tables, too, were elegant and ingenious; some had mechanical fittings that raised up compartments for paint, powder and patches or slid out platforms and drawers when the top was raised. Many designs had adjustable mirrors that lifted up and could be set at an angle. Lowboy was the American term for a dressing table with drawers which could act as a base for a high chest or highboy.

There were other types of table that served less of a practical, more of an architectural purpose. The console table was not free-standing but fixed to the wall by a pair of bracket-like legs that supported the top, which was usually of marble. The base of the console table was liable to be highly ornate, carved and gilded in a manner sympathetic to the style of chim-

neypiece or wall decoration. Pier tables, which were not fixed to the wall but stood against it, took their name from the term for the section of supporting wall – the pier – between two windows; pier tables were invariably combined with mirrors. The practice of placing mirrors between pairs of windows was well-established and contributed to the symmetry of the room as well as increasing the sense of light and space. Other tables intended to be placed against the wall were usually left with their backs unfinished and undecorated.

Table legs followed the same progression in design as those on chairs, with the cabriole form of the beginning of the century giving way to tapering square sectioned legs (also known as Marlborough legs, after the 4th Duke who commissioned much furniture from Ince and Mayhew). Exceptionally slender legs were a feature of turn-of-the-century pieces.

Top: Design for a console table in oak, with inlays of sycamore.
Above: Detail of the Linley Classic console table.

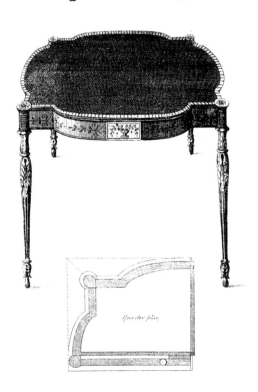

Left: A design for a Pembroke table by Hepplewhite. These light, portable tables, also known in the eighteenth century as Universal tables, generally had a drawer or drawers under the top and flaps which folded out on hinged brackets. They were often used as breakfast tables.

Sheraton attributes the name to the Countess of Pembroke, 'the lady who first gave orders for one of them'.

Below left: Card games were a popular pursuit and pattern books often featured designs for special card tables with green baize tops, such as this example by Sheraton.

Below: One of a pair, this George III side table in satinwood has rosewood crossbanding and inlay of husks, halved lunettes and ribbon-tied swags, with urn lunettes on the frieze.

Left: A Sheraton rectangular Pembroke table. This example has oval panels of burr yew wood within borders of mahogany and is crossbanded in kingwood. The tapering legs are fitted with leather castors.

Below: The centre table is a design associated with the end of the period, when furniture arrangement began to become more fixed. The beautiful top of this Regency table is of pollard oak, banded with ebony – the use of native woods was pioneered by George Bullock, a famous Regency maker. The triangular base has a frieze of Vitruvian scrolls and ormolu paw feet cast with lotus-leaves and anthemia.

Below: A Chippendale design for a sideboard table, with suggested variations for decorative treatment. Such pieces, which stood against the wall, were often left unfinished at the back.

Right: Work tables, special tables for embroidery and needlework, were often highly decorative. This French example in tulipwood, inlaid with sycamore and with gilt bronze mounts, dates from around 1785. The top is set with Sèvres porcelain.

Above: The sofa table appeared towards the end of the eighteenth century. Designed to be placed in front of a sofa to cater for a variety of occasional uses, the sofa table is generally long and narrow, with flaps at either end. This Regency sofa table is in mahogany.

Below: Exceptionally delicate, these Sheraton work tables in rosewood stand on slender tapering curved legs. The octagonal tops feature scenes in 'grisaille' (tones of grey).

Drum tables, occasionally used for writing, were more often centrally placed in a hall. Drawers in the circumference were often used for filing papers and the top sometimes rotated. This fine Regency brass-inlaid rosewood version has four working drawers flanked by three false ones, together with a fitted pen drawer. The top is supported by a central turned shaft on a concave-sided platform base; the claw feet are in giltmetal.

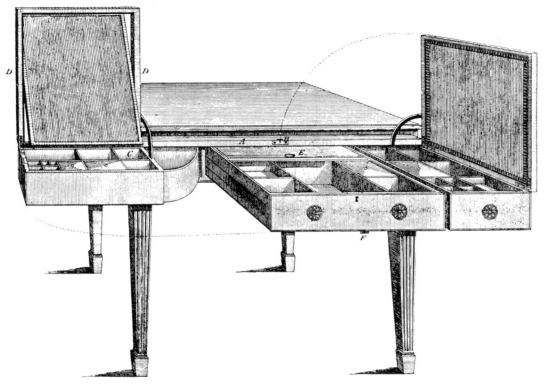

The ingenuity of eighteenth-century design and care for detail is evident in furniture created for dressing and the toilet. A typical example is Rudd's table, a 'reflecting' dressing table design of 1788 from Hepplewhite's 'Guide'. It is not known to whom the table owes its name, but it was described as 'the most complete dressing table made, possessing every convenience which can be wanted, or mechanism and ingenuity supply'. Equipped with a myriad of compartments and receptacles for paint, patches, jewels and all the accoutrements of style, it reflects the great importance attached to personal appearance by gentlemen and ladies alike.

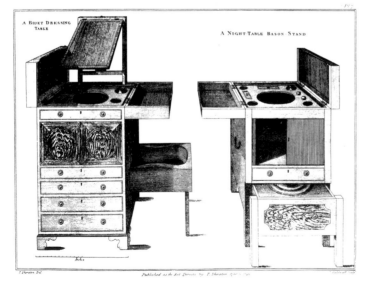

Other furniture for the toilet includes such pieces as the 'bidet dressing table' and 'night-table bason-stand' (designs by Sheraton, far left) and the shaving table (design by Hepplewhite, left).
Rather more compact than most dressing table designs, these items show that washing was still rather less important than dressing and making up.

Left: A superb early nineteenth-century chess table features scenes from Piranesi's engravings in the white squares.

Below: The sycamore games table by David Linley Furniture incorporates a covering lid and has a backgammon board in marquetry.

DINING FURNITURE

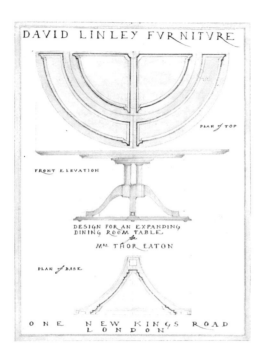

Tables and other pieces of furniture associated with dining underwent considerable development during the eighteenth century. At the beginning of the period, it was more usual for dining to take place at one or a number of small gateleg tables that could be set up easily for a meal and taken away again afterwards. By the end of the century, the dining table, having seen significant changes in design, was more likely to have a fixed location and to be accompanied by a number of other convenient accessories that made serving more efficient and the experience of dining more comfortable.

Drop-leaf tables were an early improvement on the

gateleg: the absence of stretchers and fewer legs made them more comfortable. From the 1760s on, larger tables were made by fitting a pair of D-shaped tables at either end of a drop-leaf, although there were still too many legs for comfort. The answer came in the form of the pedestal base, introduced in the 1780s. Between two and four pedestals supported a number of leaves, depending on the size required; chairs could be freely drawn up to the table without encountering the obstacle of a leg. Pembroke tables and single pedestal breakfast tables continued to be used in less formal circumstances.

The other major innovation of the period was the sideboard. Serving tables, a form of side table, were large tables with marble or wooden tops but without drawers. Adam's contribution was to add a pair of flanking pedestals, surmounted by urns, as well as other accessories designed en suite, such as wine coolers. Urns with spouts held iced drinking water or washing water; others were fitted with compartments for knives. This serving ensemble was simplified by Hepplewhite and made more compact, with integral drawers for cutlery and glasses, and cupboards, sometimes lined in lead, so that crushed ice could be packed around wine to keep it cool. Cellarets on stands and wine coolers which sat under the sideboard were similarly fitted. A deep drawer might also be lined in lead so that it could be

Far left: A design for an expandable dining table, with a removable outer ring. Left: In English oak, ebony inlay and sycamore bandings this dining table by David Linley Furniture has an air of permanence and solidity without appearing too monumental. Legs are comfortably out of the way.

filled with water and used to wash glasses between courses. Altogether, the sideboard was an imposing piece, adding to the grandeur of dining while contributing to the ease and speed of service.

The dumb waiter was another important dining accessory, dating from 1740. It consisted of a three-tiered stand which stood alongside the dining table and enabled those at table to help themselves to small dishes from its revolving trays. The dumb waiter, as its name suggests, allowed meals to proceed without the constant attendance of servants, an advantage if one was dining intimately or informally. Speeding the circulation of wine and beer was another preoccupation. Beer wagons and wine waiters were trolleys which moved along the floor; there were also coasters which slid bottles along on the table top.

Above: One of our first commissions and our only mahogany piece, this dining table was commissioned by a client with a passion for the Gothic. The leg supports echo the design of a window in the room for which the table was designed.

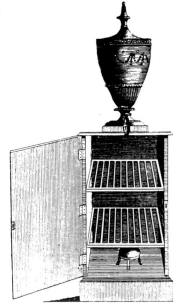

Right: Hepplewhite design for pedestal and vase shows how function was strictly concealed. The pedestal is equipped with racks for warming plates; the urn is fitted with a spout in the base for serving ice water or washing water for cutlery and glasses.

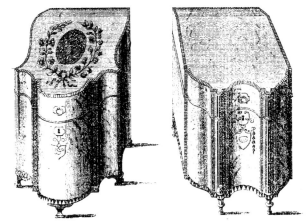

Above: Sheraton designs for knife cases, with sloping lids and small ring handles. Some urns were also fitted out as knife boxes.

Below: Cellarets or wine coolers, used for storing bottles of wine to be drunk during the course of a meal, were lead-lined and often hexagonal in shape. A tap in the base allowed water from melted ice to be drained. This example from the late eighteenth century is in satinwood, the top inlaid with scrolling leaves surrounding a central patera, urns and swags on the sides.

Left: Dating from about 1760, this English mahogany three-tiered dumbwaiter is on a tripod base. Each tier has a spindle gallery. The dumbwaiter was placed beside the dining table and held sauces and condiments for self-service.

Left: Dining tables with D-shaped ends were common from 1760 right up to the Regency period. Although this design was an improvement on the gateleg table, it was still not entirely comfortable to sit at. This Regency extending dining table in mahogany with square tapering legs is of very plain design.

Below: The pedestal dining table, introduced in the last decades of the eighteenth century, finally allowed diners to sit without awkward entanglement with table legs. Versions were made with two, three or even four pedestals, each generally with four splayed legs.

Below: Hepplewhite is particularly known for designs for sideboards and sideboard tables. The sideboard table was a descendant of the medieval serving table.

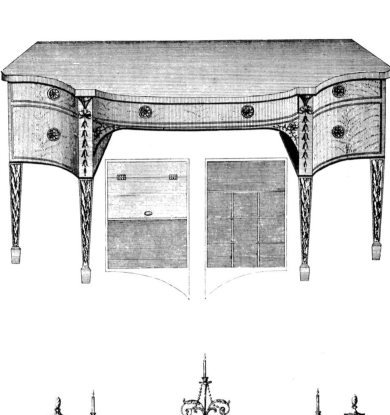

Right: By the end of the century, the sideboard had evolved into a more substantial piece incorporating cupboards and drawers for glass, cutlery and silver. This relatively simple design is by Hepplewhite.

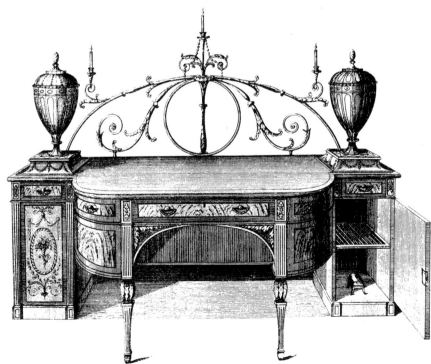

Right: In this Sheraton sideboard, all the dining accessories have fused into a single piece. The table has drawers and the pedestals and urns are incorporated within the design rather than being separate free-standing elements as they were formerly. Here the urns are fitted out for use as knife cases.

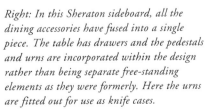

WRITING FURNITURE

Above: The Venetian desk by David Linley Furniture incorporates filing drawers and a keyboard surface which springs out at a touch.
Right: The sycamore pen cabinet holds 300 pens in four drawers, with a secret drawer hidden in the base. Indian rosewood handles are in the shape of pen nibs.

Letterwriting in the eighteenth century was far from the prosaic activity it is today. For a member of fashionable society it was not enough to be elegantly dressed and live in tasteful surroundings; equally important was the ability to display a lively wit, to be well read in the classics, and conversant with the latest amusements. Before mass media and instant communication, letterwriting was the common means of keeping up with the news but it also gave the opportunity to display one's learning and refined sensibilities. Both sexes maintained lengthy and varied correspondences and to

be a good letterwriter, in the manner of Lady Mary Wortley Montagu, was a valued accomplishment.

Writing furniture shows the importance attached to this activity. There were many different forms of writing desk and table devised during the century, some specifically for women. Desks were not restricted to libraries or drawing rooms but were often found in dining rooms and boudoirs. Writing tables, with flat tops and drawers, were elegant pieces dating from the latter part of the period. The *bonheur-du-jour* was a popular form of ladies' writing table. Particularly refined was the Carlton House table, designed for the Prince Regent, with a low curved bank of small drawers surrounding the writing surface.

More substantial were pedestal and kneehole desks, with banks of drawers flanking a recess and a plain or tooled leather top. Library tables could also be quite grand affairs and were usually placed centrally in a library. These generally stood on a central pedestal and might have drawers in the circumference.

Throughout the eighteenth century and well into the nineteenth, one of the most popular pieces of writing furniture was the bureau, a chest of drawers with a hinged flap that let down to form a writing surface. The interior was usually fitted with compartments,  pigeonholes and sometimes small drawers for writing materials. The fall-front design where the flap was supported on sliding rails called 'lopers' was succeeded by the tambour front which rolled up, with a flap that slid out to form the writing surface.

An ingenious and space saving arrangement was to

A desk by David Linley Furniture in harewood and sycamore, with marquetry designs of dolphins and opening door fronts on each side.

combine a bureau with a bookcase or cabinet. Bureau-bookcases and secretaire-cabinets were made in two pieces, the upper bookcase or cabinet fitting into the top of the bureau. Secretaires did not have slant fronts; instead the front of the top drawer extended to make a writing surface. The tops of such pieces expressed a range of architectural themes: the 'bonnet' top was popular in America, while broken pediments and deep cornices gave a classical flavour. The doors might be panelled, mirrored or glazed in patterns that recalled the design of sash windows, or in more fanciful Gothick and Chinoiserie styles.

The Carlton House writing table was a form of desk first designed for the Prince of Wales, later George IV, for his personal use at Carlton House. In satinwood, with a curved bank of drawers and a lifting book rest, this desk features silver handles bearing the Prince's coronet; the tapered legs also have silver castors.

A 1760 design for a writing desk by Chippendale; the lefthand cupboard was probably intended for storing books. The serpentine curves show the influence of the Rococo.

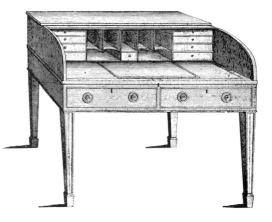

Above: Tambour fronts were common from the late eighteenth century on. This writing table by Hepplewhite is commendably practical and restrained in design.

Below: The kneehole desk first appeared at the beginning of the eighteenth century and often features a cupboard in the kneehole with banks of drawers on either side.

George III satinwood cylinder bureau with a rising desk, and an array of drawers and compartments. The tambour front rolls up to allow the writing surface to be pulled out.

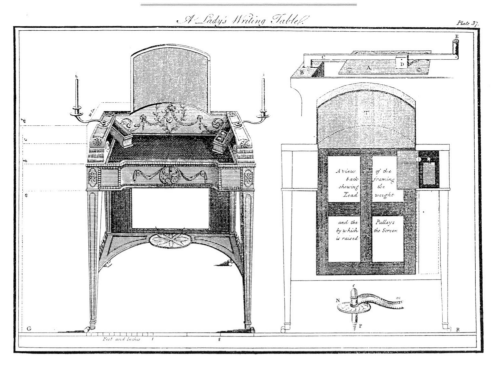

Writing furniture designed specifically for ladies was light and graceful; writing tables and small desks were often placed in bedrooms and boudoirs. This Sheraton design incorporates candleholders and a counterbalanced screen raised by pulleys to protect the face while writing in front of a fire. Drawers for ink and pens spring out when the base of the candle branch is pressed.

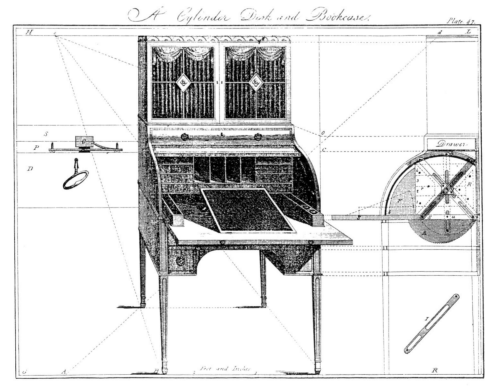

A design for a 'cylinder' desk and bookcase by Sheraton, with pleated green silk behind the glass doors of the bookcase. Such compact pieces, intricately fitted and detailed, reflect a need to save space as well as a taste for elegance and refinement. In this design, the mechanism of the 'cylinder' or tambour and the slide are linked so that they operate together.

Opposite: The 'bonheur-du-jour' was a form of ladies' writing desk that originated in France. This sumptuous example, in mahogany with ormolu mounts, is thought to be by John Okeley in the style of Röentgen. It has three tambours, the central one enclosing pigeonholes and a drawer, the flanking two enclosing spring-operated cupboards which in turn enclose an intricate arrangement of drawers. The top lifts up to reveal a mirror and there are leather-lined slides in the frieze. The three flights of 'steps' are each fitted as a drawer.

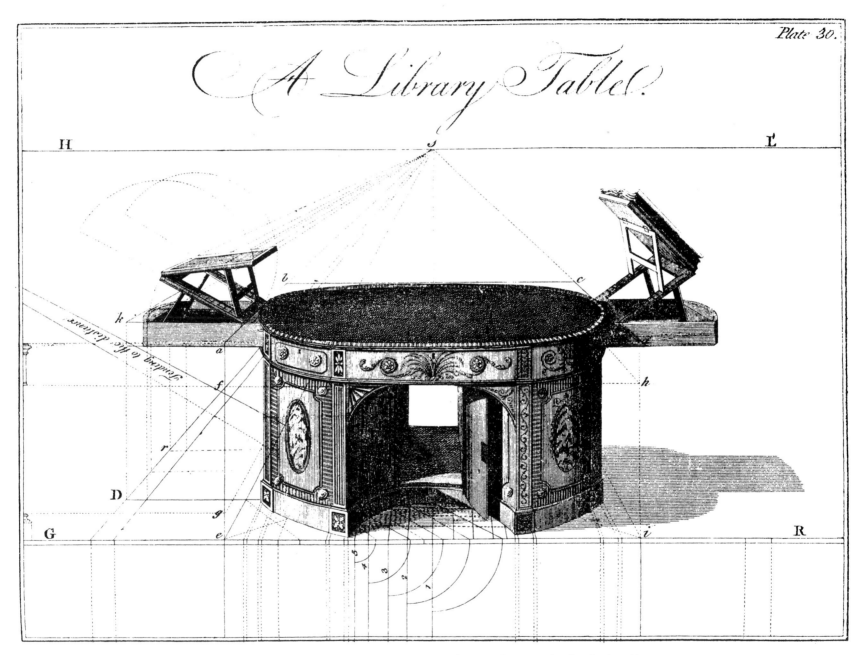

Plate 30.

A Library Table.

*Design for a library table by Sheraton. Drawers in the circumference are fitted with adjustable
desks. Library tables were often fitted with leather tops.*

A KIDNEY TABLE

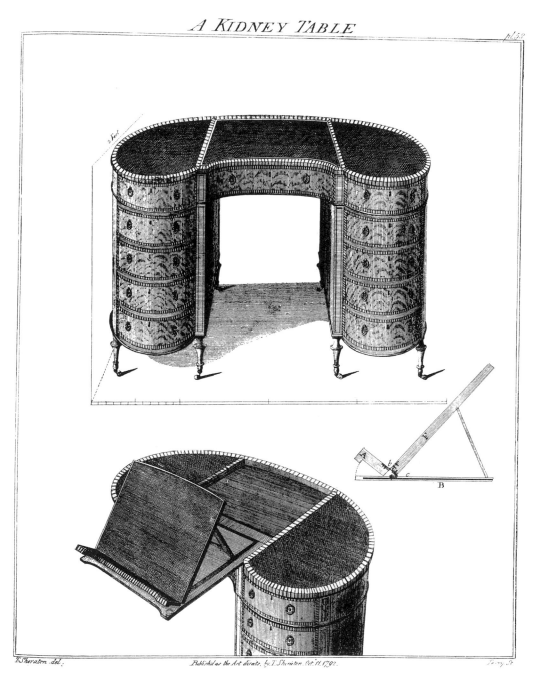

A kneehole 'Kidney table' by Sheraton, with a pull-out desk. The introduction of the kidney shape is particularly associated with Sheraton.

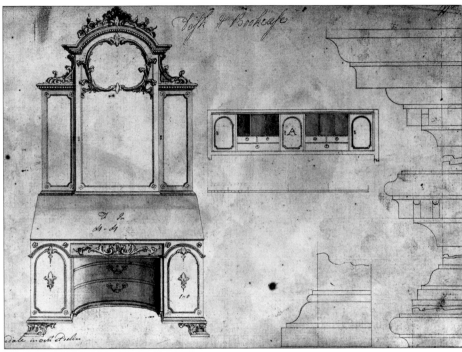

Above: 'Desk and bookcase' was the term used by both Chippendale and Hepplewhite for 'bureau bookcase', a combination of a slant front bureau, with a flap that let down as a writing surface, and a bookcase with doors, glazed, solid or mirrored, which rested on the bureau. This Chippendale design with mirrored doors is embellished with rich carving in a medley of styles.

Right: This mahogany and white pine desk and bookcase is attributed to the workshop of Nathaniel Gould (1734–82), Salem, Massachusetts and dates from around 1779. The 'bonnet' top is characteristic of American designs.

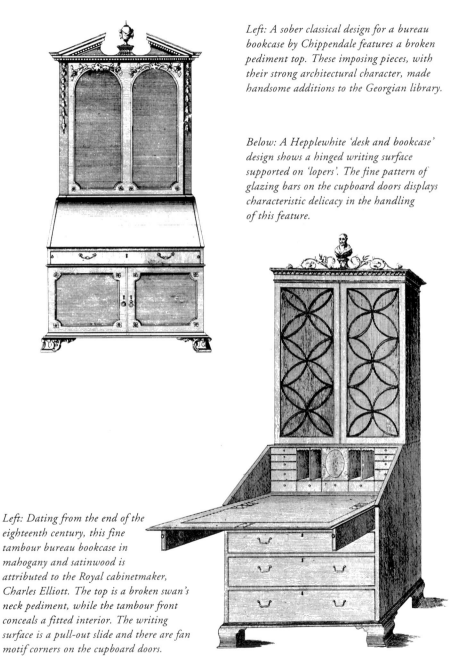

Left: A sober classical design for a bureau bookcase by Chippendale features a broken pediment top. These imposing pieces, with their strong architectural character, made handsome additions to the Georgian library.

Below: A Hepplewhite 'desk and bookcase' design shows a hinged writing surface supported on 'lopers'. The fine pattern of glazing bars on the cupboard doors displays characteristic delicacy in the handling of this feature.

Left: Dating from the end of the eighteenth century, this fine tambour bureau bookcase in mahogany and satinwood is attributed to the Royal cabinetmaker, Charles Elliott. The top is a broken swan's neck pediment, while the tambour front conceals a fitted interior. The writing surface is a pull-out slide and there are fan motif corners on the cupboard doors.

CASE FURNITURE

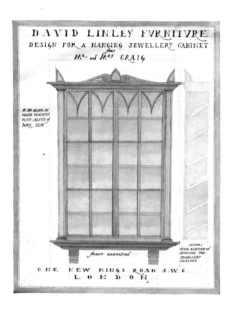

*Above: Design for a necklace cabinet by David Linley Furniture, in
walnut and inlaid with Madrona burr, Swiss pear and ebony.
Right: Made by David Linley Furniture in sycamore, Swiss pear, ebony
and harewood, this cabinet was designed to house a television.*

As life grew more comfortable and possessions
accumulated, there was a greater need for items
of furniture in which to keep things. 'Case' furniture
is a broad term which encompasses a wide range of
essentially storage pieces, from chests of drawers to
commodes and bookcases.

Chests of drawers took over from simple chests in
the late seventeenth century as the principal means of
tidying and organizing household goods. Plain and
utilitarian or sumptuously enriched with matched
veneers and crossbanding, the chest of drawers was an
indispensable bedroom and dressing room piece.

Block fronts were typical of New England chests of
drawers, while bow or serpentine fronts were exceed-
ingly popular in late eighteenth-century England.

Chests on chests (tallboys) and the American varia-
tion, the highboy, which stood on a stand or a lowboy
(a low table with drawers), were popular for storing
clothes until superseded by the wardrobe. In common
with many large upright pieces, the proportions and
detail generally displayed the designer's concern for
architectural correctness.

More elegantly curvaceous was the commode, a
fashionable piece of drawing room furniture introduced from France. Commodes, with bombe or serpentine fronts and decorative carving or marquetry,

were relatively low which meant they could be placed against a wall without obscuring its decoration.

In the seventeenth century, cabinets with lavish decoration and exotic use of fine materials, were commissioned to house curios and precious collections. With doors enclosing an array of smaller drawers, the larger versions stood on stands. By the eighteenth century, the collecting of fine objects – books, porcelain, bronzes, coins, medals – became less exclusively associated with the very wealthy or artistically enlightened connoisseur. When Pepys commissioned a series of tall free-standing

bookcases to house his growing library in the mid-seventeenth century, such collections were very rare. A century later, many houses included a room designated as a library, books were more plentiful and bookcases the normal means of displaying and storing them.

Like Pepys' earlier models, these were often 'architectural' in form, with solid cupboard bases and upper shelves generally enclosed with glazed doors. Many larger bookcases were of the breakfront type, with a projecting central section. The tops were often in the form of a broken pediment and urn. Very similar to bookcases were display cabinets for storing porcelain services and other decorative pieces. Dwarf bookcases and other small elegant designs from the Regency period reflect the need to save space.

Top: Oak bookcase designed for David Linley. Above: This magnificent breakfront bookcase is clearly architectural in character, with its broken pediment top and classically inspired proportions.

Below: Possibly by Ince and Mayhew, and dating from around 1775, this satinwood commode features a fan pattern in marquetry on the top surrounded by swags, *bows and medallions, and front and sides inlaid with other neoclassical motifs. There is a central drawer over a bowed cupboard.*

Right: A Chippendale drawing for a serpentine-front commode. The curvaceous form of the commode was introduced to England from France in the mid-eighteenth century and quickly became a most fashionable item.

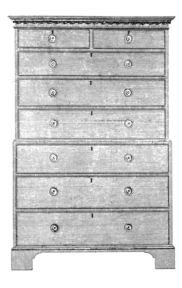

Below: One of a pair of Chippendale serpentine commodes in mahogany, with four drawers of graduated depth and a pull-out slide. The carving on the corners is applied and features flowers, foliage and scrolls. The piece dates from around 1760.

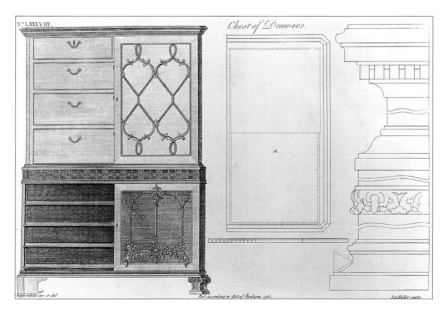

Above left and centre: Two Hepplewhite designs for 'double chest of drawers' or chest on chests, from the 'Cabinet-Maker and Upholsterer's Guide'.
Above right: Most chest on chests were made in mahogany after 1735, as is this example which dates from around 1770.

A Chippendale design for a chest of drawers with sliding shelves for storing clothes, from the first edition of the 'Director', 1754, featuring different door designs.

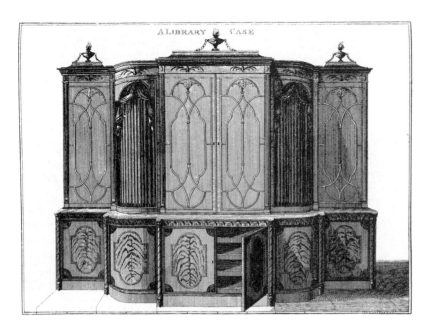

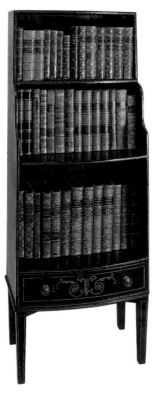

Above: A design for a 'Library Case' by Sheraton, with shelves in the central base cupboard for storing clothes. By the end of the century, the library was generously furnished, lined with books and equipped with desks, library table, reading chairs and easy chairs. The dignity of furnishings and decoration reflected the library's traditional designation as a 'masculine' enclave.

Right: Space-saving was increasingly a concern in the Regency period. This Sheraton-style painted pine bookcase holds a small collection of books. There were other designs for movable bookcases, 'small open shelves for books under present reading, and which a lady can move to any sitting room'.

Far right: This magnificent early nineteenth-century bookcase relates to a design published in Sheraton's 'Encyclopedia', 1806.

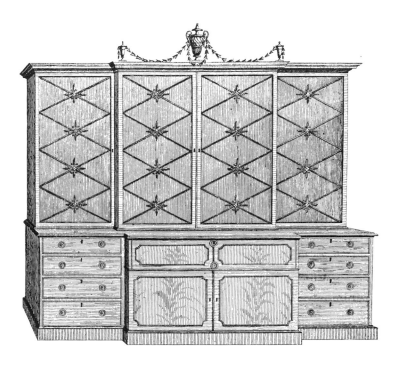

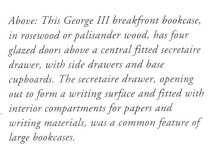

Above: This George III breakfront bookcase, in rosewood or palisander wood, has four glazed doors above a central fitted secretaire drawer, with side drawers and base cupboards. The secretaire drawer, opening out to form a writing surface and fitted with interior compartments for papers and writing materials, was a common feature of large bookcases.

Above right: A Hepplewhite 'Library Case' design also incorporates a secretaire drawer, flanking drawers and base cupboards. Great attention has been paid to the elegant design of the glazing bars in the upper bookcase. The wardrobe evolved from the earlier linen press.

Right: This Sheraton design incorporates cupboards, shelves and drawers for storing, folding and hanging clothes.

BEDS

In the words of John Gloag, eighteenth-century beds were a 'minor exercise in architectural composition'. The State Bed designed by Robert Adam for Osterley Park provides ample justification for this statement, with its four bed posts in the form of columns supporting a magnificently decorated classical dome.

Beds had long been a significant and often monumental item of furniture. Lavish hangings and testers proclaimed the wealth and status of a household; in the seventeenth century the chief use of fabric in the interior was as bed coverings and drapery, providing much-needed warmth and privacy.

The eighteenth century saw the wooden frame become visible and decorative once more. The frieze and cornice of the tester followed the architectural orders; bed posts were often in the form of columns. State beds, often set into alcoves, fell under the architect's design control, while their furnishings were the preserve of the upholsterer.

Particularly extravagant canopies and hangings in countless permutations were fashionable in France; romantically contrived effects with drapery remained a feature of tented Empire beds. The *lit en bateau* with shapely curved ends was a popular design dating from the end of the century.

Left: Designed and made by David Linley Furniture, Elton John's bedroom features a fitted architectural screen of English facades which encloses the bed and incorporates night tables and chests of drawers. Swiss pear is the predominant wood, with inlays of sycamore and ebony.
Below: The State Bed at Houghton, 1732, has been described as the most sumptuous single piece of furniture ever designed by William Kent.

Opposite: Robert Adam's design for the State Bed at Osterley Park for Robert Child, a wealthy banker, was inspired by an engraving of a classical temple at Baalbec and featured a dome and eight columns. It was made in 1776 by John Linnell and was exceptionally expensive.

The Empress Josephine's bed at Malmaison c.1810 was designed by Percier and Fontaine, the most influential designers of the Empire period, and made by Jacob Desmalter.

A design for a bed by Sheraton shows drapery in the French style framing a couch, the fabric caught up to either side in soft folds.

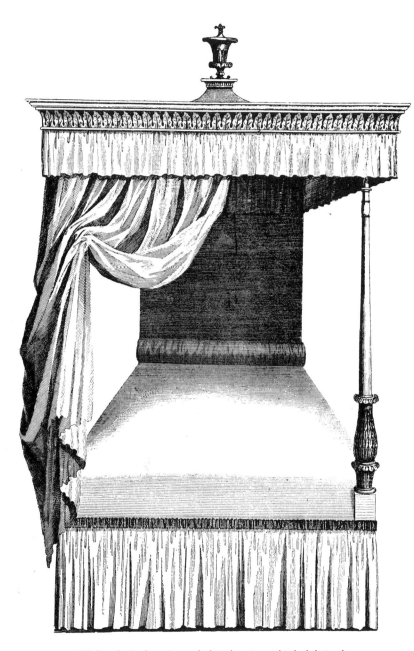

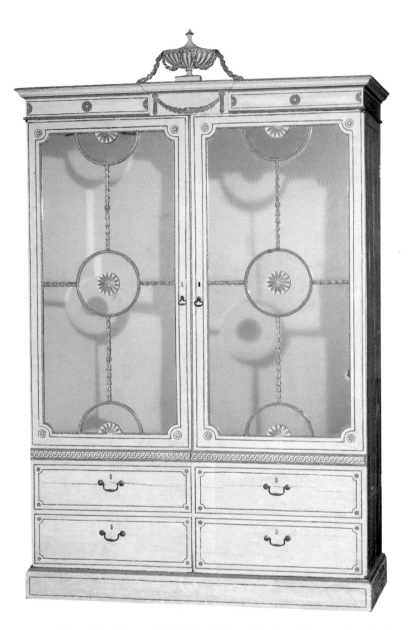

With a classical cornice and plain hangings, this bed design by Hepplewhite is a model of elegant sobriety.

A press bed made by Chippendale for David Garrick's villa at Hampton. Press beds folded away into cupboards which were made to look like wardrobes.

MISCELLANEOUS ITEMS

A jewellery box by David Linley Furniture in walnut, ebony and sycamore, with a mirror built in under the lid.

The skills of craftsmen and ingenuity of designers were expressed in numerous other articles and pieces of furniture, many of which were intensely practical. Yet however practical, problems of use and function were solved with the usual elegance and attention to form.

Accessories for tea drinking included caddies and trays. Caddies, lockable boxes sometimes fitted with integral compartments for different types of tea and for sugar, reflect the high price of tea and the need to keep supplies secure. Many examples were veneered or beautifully decorated with marquetry and crossband-

ing. Trays, with galleries, oval or rectangular in shape, were similarly embellished, inlaid with floral or classical designs.

Adjustable stands for music, dating from the end of the century, often incorporated musical motifs, such as lyre shapes. Low canterburies for holding music books could be slid on castors under the piano when not required. Tiered revolving book-stands housing a small collection of books made a movable library. Whatnots, which first appeared at the beginning of the nineteenth century, were tiered display stands for books and objects.

Library steps, essential to reach the highest shelves of a bookcase, were often ingeniously designed so they could be concealed within other pieces of furniture, neatly folding into the top of a Pembroke table or into the form of a chair or stool. Bed steps, for clambering into the high beds of the time, were incorporated into cupboards that also held chamber pots. Folding beds, which could be packed up and moved from place to place, were a popular means of avoiding the miseries of verminous inns.

Firescreens were devised at the beginning of the eighteenth century as a way of protecting the complexion from the blazing heat of a fire. They consisted of a movable screen, usually covered with an embroidered panel, attached to a pole which was supported on a tripod base. Screens for keeping out draughts also helped to make the drawing room more comfortable.

As contemporary interiors show, the practical as well as the decorative potential of mirrors was not unappreciated. During the eighteenth century, mirrors were increasingly used in reception rooms to make the most of natural light and multiply the effect of candles and fires, as well as to contribute to the all-important sense of symmetry in arrangement. The classical sympathies of designers were betrayed in the architectural style of frames, particularly at the beginning of the period and later on, when Neoclassicism had become the dominant style. But the decoration of frames could equally be the excuse for extravagant Rococo flights of fancy in carved giltwood or fantastic Chinoiserie motifs. Oval toilet mirrors date from the late eighteenth century, when cheval glasses, movable mirrors suspended on a four-legged frame, were introduced after it became possible to cast mirror plate in larger pieces. Convex mirrors were a particular feature of Regency interiors.

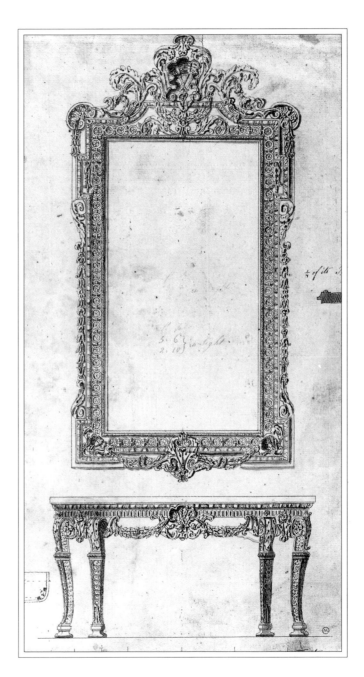

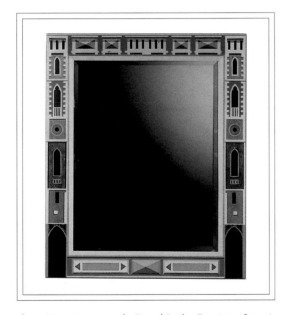

Above: Venetian mirror by David Linley Furniture featuring marquetry of architectural details.
Right: Mirrors and console tables were designed en suite, as shown in this drawing by Chippendale.

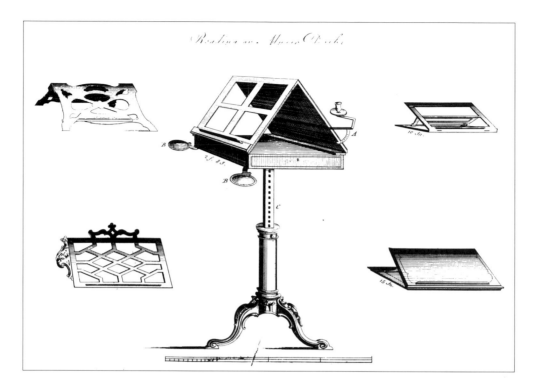

Designs for adjustable reading or music desks by Ince and Mayhew, from 'The Universal System of Household Furniture', 1760.

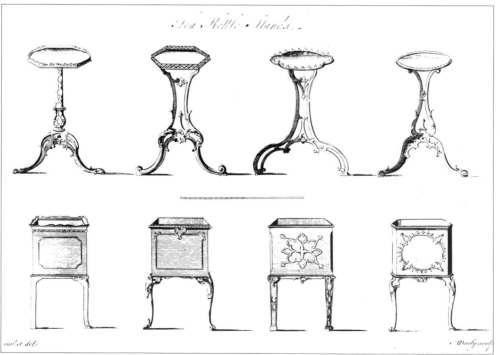

From the same source, a range of tea kettle stands, one of a host of accessories associated with the ritual of taking tea. Kettle stands often had galleried tops.

Below: The canterbury was designed to hold music books and first appeared around the end of the eighteenth century; today it is commonly put to use storing magazines and newspapers. This Regency example is in simulated rosewood.

Right: Sheraton designs for 'horse dressing glasses', mirrors on four legs. The design on the left has a comb tray, and a pin cushion on top of small boxes, which can be pushed round behind the mirror when not in use. The design on the right incorporates a fold-down writing table, a somewhat surprising combination of functions.

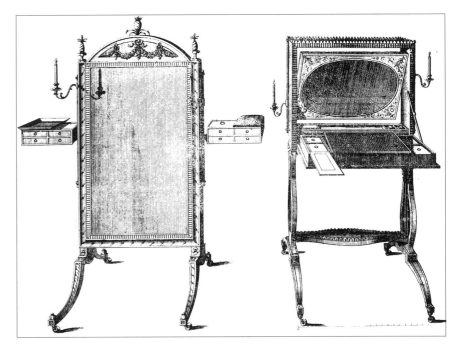

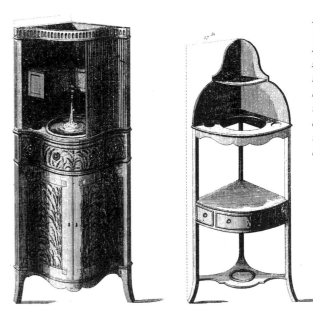

Left: These designs for 'corner bason stands' by Sheraton, held relatively small washbasins and incorporated places for holding soap and other requisites. Such pieces could 'stand in a genteel room without giving offence to the eye'.

Pole firescreens featured panels on a tripod stand that could be adjusted in height to protect the face from the heat of the fire. The panels might be wooden, framed needlework or tapestry, or painted. Two designs by Ince and Mayhew (far left); two by Hepplewhite (left).

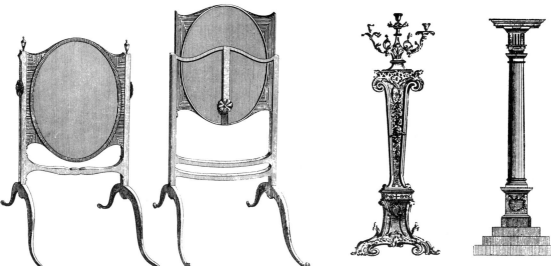

Far left: Cheval screens or 'horse fire screens' in the contemporary term, stood on four legs and could be raised or lowered like a blind, as shown in the Hepplewhite design.
Left: Two designs for candlestands by Ince and Mayhew.

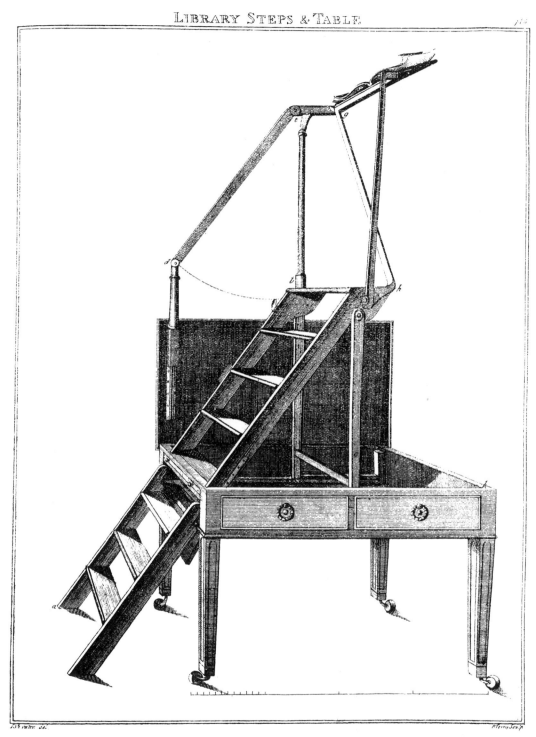

Library steps, essential for reaching the topmost shelves in a library lined with books from floor to ceiling, were generally not considered items worthy of display. Considerable ingenuity was exercised in devising steps that could be folded down when not in use and concealed within other more acceptable pieces of furniture. This Sheraton design shows steps that fold flat into the top of a library table.

The most popular style of mirror in the Regency period was the circular convex form which originated in France. This ebonized and gilded example has candle arms and hanging glass drops to reflect the light.

Above: Eighteenth-century girandoles were large carved and gilded sconces with Rococo framing, often backed with mirror to multiply the effect of candlelight. This design is by Chippendale.

Opposite left: One of a pair of George III giltwood mirrors by Chippendale for Harewood House. The frame is edged with husks and egg-and-dart ornament. The cresting consists of an urn supported by scrolled acanthus, framing anthemions.

Opposite right: Supremely architectural in form, with columns supporting a broken swan's neck pediment, this Irish George III giltwood pierglass is by John and William Booker of Dublin.

CHAPTER FIVE

ARRANGEMENT AND DISPLAY

An appreciation of classical furniture naturally awakens interest in how rooms were arranged and used in the past. The eighteenth century was a period of change in interior decoration, when rigid formalities were beginning to give way to notions of comfort and convenience. The placing of furniture was important in how these changes were expressed.

Scholarly experts in historical decoration are reluctant to assign a particular 'style' to a period and remind us that at any given time examples of quite different types of decoration can be found happily coexisting. And we must always be aware of our own preconceptions – perhaps drawn from visits to country houses, museum collections or even the cinema – which colour our expectations. With all these reservations in

mind, it is nevertheless worth trying to form some picture of eighteenth-century rooms and their original furnishings.

Over the past decade there has been considerable interest in recreating period decor, in varying degrees of accuracy. The great English decorator John Fowler always emphasized that restoration inevitably means reinterpretation, even when it arises from the most rigorous academic research. Too great a concern for period accuracy can produce rather stilted results which can be as 'wrong' in their own way as more flamboyant interpretations of mood and flavour. But these vexed issues principally apply to the restoration of interiors of national cultural interest. For most people today, the main question is how to combine old and new sympathetically.

Above: The New House, Sussex, designed by John Outram shows a 'post-modern' approach to the design of the interior, using classical elements in a contemporary way.

Clavis desk with burr oak top and bandings in ebony and sycamore is framed by a collection of tree prints.

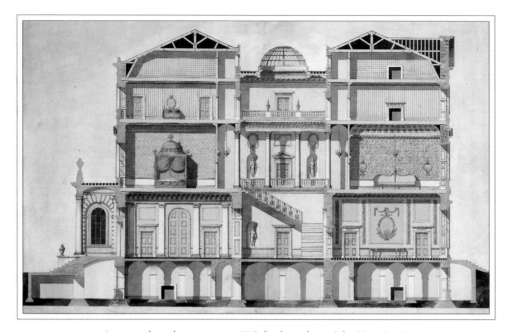

A section through a mansion, 1774, by the architect John Yenn (1750-1821). The furniture shown would be designed by the architect.

USE AND ARRANGEMENT

A sequence of richly appointed anterooms culminating in the magnificent display of a state bedroom formed the central core of a great seventeenth- century house. It is almost impossible today to appreciate the full social significance of this type of planning or to understand the ceremonial importance of a state bed, by far the most expensive item in a great household. A procession of sumptuous state apartments was the ultimate status symbol, tangible proof that one could accommodate a sovereign or noble guest. In this context, a state bedroom was not a private domain but instead represented the focus of power and authority.

By the middle of the eighteenth century, changes were underway that would eventually bring about the type of room use and arrangement with which we are familiar today. Rooms of 'parade', as state apartments were known, did not disappear from the planning of great houses; the first floor or piano nobile was often devoted to such a formal sequence. But with increased wealth, leisure and gentility, there was a need for more relaxed and open ways of living. The classical villa, rather than the palace, was admirably suited to this shift in manners and taste.

There was a need to accommodate different activities and rooms gradually began to be more fixed in function. Rooms for music or billiards, galleries for pictures or sculpture, and libraries for reading appeared

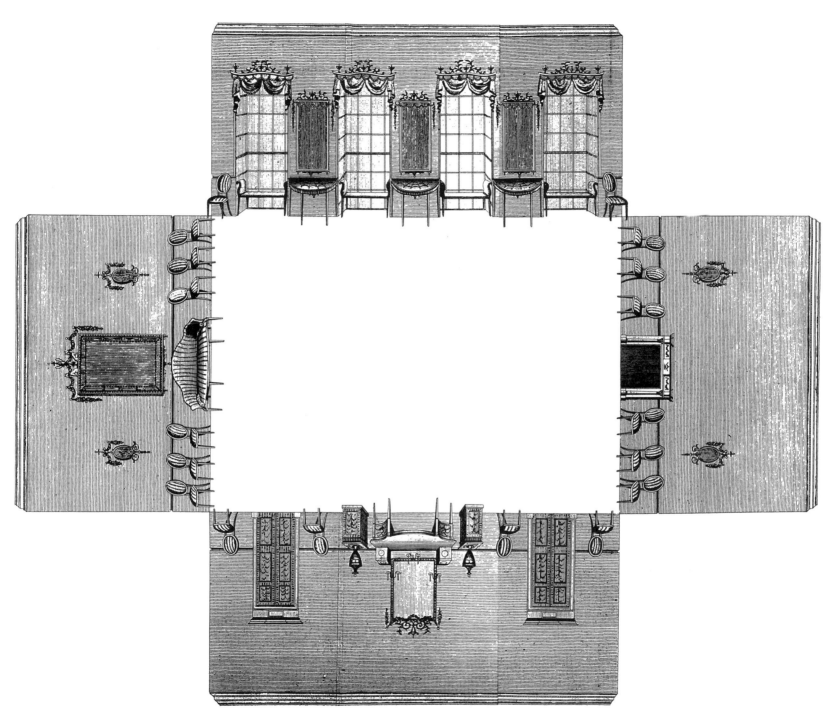

*A plan of a room, from Hepplewhite's 'Guide' of 1788, showing
the 'proper distribution of the Furniture'.*

during the course of the century, reflecting new interests, accomplishments and possessions. It was increasingly fashionable to entertain in larger numbers and a saloon, or room for company, was often present as well as a drawing room. A separate room for dining, first known in seventeenth-century France, was not common until the late eighteenth century when large dining tables, which necessarily had to remain fixed in position, were introduced. By then it was beginning to become the fashion to dine later.

The sparseness of most eighteenth-century rooms often comes as a shock to those who expect to see historic houses cluttered with the accumulated treasures of generations. To modern eyes, this restraint in furnishing and delight in space and architecture can be very refreshing, especially when compared with the gaudy showiness and overpowering density of many Victorian interiors. What makes the contrast even more striking is the formality of arrangement. In the eighteenth century, few pieces of furniture stood away from the wall unless in active use. Tables, chairs and sofas were ranged around the perimeter of the room, along with larger pieces of furniture such as commodes, chests and cabinets.

This formality persisted until late in the eighteenth century. Sofas, generally one on each side of the fire, were left in place; side chairs were drawn into the room to form a sitting circle for conversation. Lightweight tables were placed as need and occasion demanded. At the end of the day, servants returned all the pieces to their accustomed positions, and sometimes withdrew items from the room altogether.

Gradually, however, these rigid symmetries gave way to a more informal spirit. By the end of the century, furniture began to be left out in the room, arranged in conversation groups. A large central table was a new feature of the drawing room, a place for writing, working, reading or eating. The new type of picturesque arrangement allowed different activities to take place comfortably and companionably in different parts of the same room. Living apartments were increasingly located at ground floor level, reflecting the desire to provide an easy connection with the landscape outside.

At the time, the change was startling enough to provoke comment and criticism. A common complaint was that the new informality made rooms look like cabinetmakers' shops, while Jane Austen described the style as creating 'a proper air of confusion'.

Written accounts, architects' plans, contemporary representations – such as the backgrounds of portraits and conversation piece pictures – together with paint samples, scraps of fabric, trimming and paper have allowed historians to build up an increasingly detailed picture of how most eighteenth-century rooms were arranged, decorated and furnished. Other factors affected the way such rooms were perceived and used, notably the level of light and the supply of heat.

Modern technology, which has given us bright, reliable lighting at the flick of a switch and uniformly heated houses even in the depths of winter, has made it easy to take such comforts for granted and hard to imagine what life would be like without them. It is difficult to appreciate just how dark most eighteenth-century rooms were after nightfall, or how cold and damp they were outside the summer months.

Candles, especially those made of beeswax, were an expensive commodity and few could afford to burn

*The Music Room at Malmaison, 1812-32, by Garneray. This Empire room, with its
neoclassical furniture shows the light drapery characteristic of the style.*

very many at a time. Even in grand houses, chandeliers went unlit year after year; glittering occasions when dozens of candles blazed in sconces and candelabra were sufficiently rare to excite much comment and wonder. Cheaper tallow candles (made of rendered animal fat) smoked and guttered, giving an uneven, flickering light. The use of gilt and mirror, which contributed so much richness to eighteenth-century interiors, had a practical side, serving to reflect and spread what little light was available around the room. Fine work and close study often had to be carried out by daylight; the tall windows that grace Georgian elevations flooded rooms with natural light.

Firelight helped to alleviate the gloom on cold nights but, owing to poorly designed chimneys and grates, the fireplace was an inefficient source of warmth. Away from the immediate fireside, where the blast of heat thrown off threatened to roast the complexion (and melt the paint on ladies' faces), rooms were uncomfortably damp and draughty. Firescreens to shield the face and standing screens to retain as much heat as possible within the sitting area, as well as padded and layered clothing, helped to compensate to some extent, but most English houses were notoriously cold and uncomfortable. On the Continent, the widespread practice of heating houses with stoves made a significant difference, yet the custom was never adopted in the British Isles.

The twin focal points of physical comfort and practicality, the fireplace and window, had some part to play in the peripatetic nature of eighteenth-century arrangement. It was an obvious advantage for furniture in everyday use to be light and portable. A writing table could be moved to the window during the daytime to make the most of the light, or a card table set up in the evening near the fire's glow.

A console table by David Linley Furniture, with an array of walnut and sycamore candlesticks. Varying the height of the candles makes a lively display.

UNITY IN THE INTERIOR

Formal arrangement was not merely a matter of social use and etiquette: it was a natural consequence of the classical system of design. Each piece of furniture had a precise location, planned with as much care as the position of integral features such as windows, fireplaces and doors. The concept of unity extended beyond architectural treatment and arrangement to colour, decoration and detail.

In France there was a clear distinction between *chaises courantes,* or movable chairs, and *chaises meublantes,* or those conceived as part of the fixed decor. On a famous occasion, Madame de Maintenon was reprimanded by Louis XIV for pulling a chair away from the wall and 'spoiling the architecture'. The carving of chair backs and seat rails, the fabric used to cover seat furniture and even the style of nailing indicates that such pieces were intended by the designer to be read as part of the wall decoration, in close harmony with it. The marble of table tops and commodes echoed the marble used in chimney pieces, the lines of sofa backs followed the curves of the panelling. Every element in a room contributed to the creation of a sense of unity and proportion.

The classical system of proportion was implicit in the way surfaces were organized. Walls were treated as miniature temple facades, with the skirting corresponding to the pedestal, the main wall area equivalent to the column and the cornice and frieze matching the entablature. These basic divisions can be seen whether the wall was panelled in wood, hung with fabric, papered or painted. And it was emphasized by certain decorating conventions, where the skirting was gener-

*The Dining Room at Osterley Park, designed by Robert Adam, in an arrangement
which shows what the room might have looked like when actually in use.*

ally painted in a dark tone and the cornice was painted in with the wall, rather than the ceiling as is more usual today.

Matching fabrics and colours within a room reinforced the architectural harmony. Coordinating colour and pattern has been enthusiastically promoted in recent times by modern manufacturers but it is an old idea, as might be guessed by the number of rooms which were known by the predominant colour of their furnishings. Daniel Marot was a pioneer of this type of unified decoration, and it was a principle to which designers and decorators of classical interiors adhered for much of the eighteenth century.

With the centre of the floor clear of furniture and a careful coordination of fabric, colour and detail, the architecture of a room could be admired in all its finesse and exquisite proportion. The wonderful painted ceilings which are characteristic of Adam's interiors were echoed in the carpets he designed to accompany them, a harmony of design which could only be appreciated in such formally arranged settings.

The brilliance and intensity of much historic decor comes as another revelation. The visual impact of an eighteenth-century interior with newly restored paintwork can be compared to seeing an old painting cleaned of the layers of discoloured varnish which have distorted its original tonal values over the years. At the same time, colour was handled with infinite subtlety, despite a rather limited palette, to create variations of texture and finish that are difficult to appreciate, much less reproduce, today.

Bright, strong colour was always associated with richness and luxury and reserved for the best rooms, for the very good reason that it was expensive, the product of rare or costly pigments and dyes; the more muted everyday shades were derived from cheaper natural earth and vegetable colours and encompassed a variety of soft greys, browns, dull greens and buffs. It was not until the nineteenth century and the invention of synthetic pigments and dyes that a broader range of colours became readily available and affordable.

Grand Palladian rooms at the beginning of the century were decorated in stone white picked out with gold or strong matt colours and formal patterns: crimson damask was favoured for wall hangings and was thought the ideal background for pictures. A rich green was another important colour. Panelling, especially if made of softwood, was often painted in a range of 'wood' or 'wainscot' colours: throughout the century there was a natural association of colour and material, evident again in the 'stone' colours widely used to decorate the walls of stone – or marble-floored halls. The use of colour was much more literal and less associative than it is today.

By the middle of the century, the French influence made a lighter palette fashionable: straw yellow, soft, delicate greens and pale blues echoed the pastel shades favoured by Madame de Pompadour. Neoclassicism ushered in a more expressive use of colour in the designs of Robert Adam and a wider range of shades, such as pea green, grey-greens, lilac and pink, in daring combinations. Painted furniture and a range of finishes such as marbling, graining and other simulations of luxurious materials brought a new playful spirit to interior decoration.

At the turn of the century archaeological discoveries popularized the Etruscan palette of rich Pompeiian red, ochre and black. A vibrant green was Napoleon's

The Georgian House, Charlotte Square, Edinburgh. Georgian houses were
minimally furnished compared with those a century later.
Checked linen covers protected fine upholstery from wear and fading.
The fan of pleated paper hides the empty hearth.

imperial colour and much seen in Empire interiors; while a strong clear yellow enjoyed a considerable vogue after the introduction of the synthetic chrome yellow in the 1820s. The Regency period saw colour at its most vibrant and daring.

Fabric was a vital source of colour in the interior and one of the key elements in decoration. Compared to the relatively reasonable cost of fine furniture from leading cabinetmakers, quite staggering amounts of money were spent on upholstery and other fabric furnishings (confusingly known as 'furniture' in the eighteenth century). There was nothing new in this. In

John Fowler and John Cornforth's *English Decoration in the Eighteenth Century*, the authors quote a striking example from the previous century, comparing the price Charles I paid for the Raphael Cartoons – £300 – with the massive sum of £1000, which was the cost of embroidered green satin hangings for a state bed.

Until pictures became more widely collected, patterned fabric was one of the chief means of giving a room richness, variety and depth of colour. A range of silks and woollen fabrics were used as wall and bed hangings, in festoons crowning the tops of windows and to cover seats and settees. Understandably, great care was taken to protect such expensive furnishings from the ravages of light and wear. Checked or striped linen loose covers protected upholstery, while blinds were in early use to keep sunlight from fading the fine damasks, satins and taffetas in well-appointed rooms.

The role of wallpaper in providing an economical alternative to fine textiles is clearly shown by the affinity between early designs for paper and fabric patterns. William Kent chose paper instead of cut velvet for the saloon at Kensington Palace, the first use of wallpaper in any royal building in Europe. By the middle of the century, English flock wallpaper was the rage in Parisian society, following the fashion set by Madame de Pompadour. Equally influential were the handpainted Chinese papers and their European Chinoiserie copies, which were widely available through retailers such as Chippendale. Wallpaper designs which reflected the classical influence were produced in the latter part of the century: John Baptist Jackson echoed the current fashion for print rooms and sculpture galleries in his designs which featured trompe l'oeil statuary and roundels of classical landscapes.

The Classical Spirit Revisited

The history of decoration enables us to understand the reasons for common practices and traditions in the interior, conventions which continue to influence our own taste, however unconsciously. The popularity of 'period' decoration obviously reflects a desire to keep these traditions alive.

There is no escaping the fact that we live in a modern age and have grown accustomed to its conveniences and comforts. Few people would like to live in surroundings which were authentically eighteenth century in respect of plumbing, cooking and heating. Nevertheless, there is a growing disenchantment with the type of relentless modernism which insists on making an abrupt break with the past and rules out any sense of continuity.

Combining old with new in the interior is a graceful way of reconciling tradition with progress. This approach takes more skill and probably a greater degree of confidence than meticulously recreating a textbook version of a period room, but it has more vitality, and it is also more versatile and accommodating than installing the latest off-the-peg look which will be out of fashion in a season.

A pioneer and perhaps the greatest exponent of this style of decorating was John Fowler, who made a unique contribution to the development of the English country house style with his often controversial restorations of National Trust houses, as well as much-copied schemes for private clients. By weeding out clutter and restoring original colours and furnishing styles, not pedantically but with a modern flair, he

Oak bookcases, made by David Linley Furniture, are finished with oil for a matt surface that also allows the wood to breathe. Their strong architectural character gives a comfortable room a sense of definition.

A console table and a chaise longue designed by Oliver Messel strike a note of elegance in an all-white bedroom with simple muslin window drapery.

placed the focus back on the architectural qualities of space, light and proportion. The harmony and balance of his schemes was obviously inspired by his deep knowledge of and affection for eighteenth-century decoration but the results were never slavish copies or pastiche. More importantly, these were rooms to be lived in and enjoyed.

Classical furniture often displays a surprising affinity with modern design. The clean lines, refined proportions and architectural detail of Neoclassical pieces mean that they can be combined quite successfully with modern tables and lamps, plain upholstered sofas and chairs or any type of furniture where the emphasis is on shape, line and form. Victorian furniture, by contrast, heavier, fussier and generally over-enriched with detail, seems to blend into modern settings less readily and to call for a more thoroughly period flavour in decoration. The essential simplicity of classical furniture owes much to the eighteenth-century obsession with usefulness, a sympathetic characteristic in a modern age where design has been dominated by the notion of form following function.

Scale is another important consideration. The rather monumental architectural pieces of the early part of the eighteenth century are much too large for the average modern room, and many original examples have sadly been cut down and altered to fit into smaller surroundings. But towards the end of the century, and into the Regency period, furniture became more compact. This process of scaling down reflected primarily a pressing need to save space, as population grew at a great rate, and cities, before the coming of the railways fostered suburban development, suffered overcrowding. The light, movable and finely proportioned designs from this period are well suited to modern life with its equivalent pressure on space.

Although the formal principle of clearing the centre of the room and placing furniture uniformly around the walls seems odd to us today, the sparseness of classical room arrangement is better attuned to most modern tastes than the heavy, suffocating clutter of the Victorian period. Looking back over the last two hundred years of interior decoration, it is nineteenth-century rooms which seem remote in time, while

Georgian interiors can seem distinctly familiar to us.

An awareness of symmetry in arrangement helps to give a classical flavour without inconveniencing modern needs. Balancing seating groups, pairs of chairs or pairs of sofas, is more appropriate than scattering furniture informally about the room. Objects on the mantelpiece and pictures on the wall can echo the way the room is organized. Symmetrical arrangements need a point of focus, traditionally the fireplace or a window, which provides the opportunity to bring out the inherent architectural character of a room.

It goes without saying that original architectural details in old houses should be preserved whenever possible. Twenty or thirty years ago it was routine practice to strip many old buildings of their fireplaces, dados and cornices in a misguided attempt to 'modernize' them. But architectural detail is not superfluous ornament, it serves to articulate proportion; without it, rooms look bare and characterless. It did not take very long to appreciate what had been lost, and thriving architectural salvage businesses now cater for the need to replace or restore such features. Expert advice and information is also widely available to enable the correct choice of style and material for the period in question.

In modern rooms, quite minimal suggestions of detail can be enough, such as an extra moulding along the top of a skirting. It often looks wrong to impose a period style on a room designed and built to quite different specifications. Adding a dado rail, for example, is meaningless without treating the upper and lower portions of wall in different ways, since its original function was to mark a break in the wall surface between the expensive or delicate coverings on the

An oak collector's cabinet, Linley Classic desk and plain upholstered chair make a handsome grouping. The jewellery box in the form of a house is fitted with drawers and includes a secret compartment.

upper part and more robust or easily renewable materials on the lower part.

Going along with the revival of interest in the decorative styles of the past has been a fascination with paint finishes – every conceivable technique from stencilling to stippling, ragging to sponging has found its enthusiastic supporters. Although the results can sometimes be crude, there have been many benefits, particularly a new understanding of depth and pattern in wall finishes and a renewed appreciation of the fact that most original wooden features, such as architraves, doors and shutters, were never intended to be mercilessly exposed, but were also painted.

The point about paint effects is that they provide subtle modulations of colour and unobtrusive patterning which are infinitely more alive than a flat emulsioned finish. Successive thin washes or glazes of near-shades and tones, with the top layer broken in some way to allow the background to show through, make soft and sympathetic backgrounds that incidentally improve with age. It is possible to achieve such effects with modern paints but there are new ranges on the market, authentic in colour and composition, which are particularly suitable for textured finishes.

Wallpapers and fabrics which reproduce eighteenth-century patterns are also available from many sources,

The marquetry screen by David Linley Furniture was commissioned for the VIP Lounge at Heathrow Airport, designed by Michael Manser.

although most tend to be expensive. It can be just as effective to make use of sympathetic modern prints or weaves, especially if the intention is to blend old and new. Textiles such as plain wool, slubbed raw silks and linen in understated designs work well with the lines of classical furniture.

Organizing fitted rooms such as kitchens and bathrooms can also provide the opportunity to introduce classical detail. Bathrooms are relatively recent innovations, with few decorative traditions of their own; kitchens, until well into the twentieth century, were essentially service rooms, unconsidered in decorative terms. In both cases, there is the need to integrate a range of appliances and fittings and provide adequate storage facilities.

Classical bathrooms and kitchens are obviously anachronistic, but the same principles and basic proportions displayed in eighteenth-century bureaus, secretaires and bookcases can form the basis of the design of any type of fitted storage, with bases filled with drawers or cupboards and upper cabinets treated in a more architectural fashion. The natural place to make the break between the two is at dado level, so that fitted furniture echoes the architectural detail of the room rather than competing awkwardly with it. The traditional item of kitchen storage furniture, the dresser, reproduces these basic divisions.

When commissioning fitted pieces, there is the opportunity to tailor the design precisely to what needs to be stored, with cubbyholes, compartments, drawers and shelves made to suit. The result is far more efficient, as well as more appealing, than bland standardized units which promise versatility but rarely deliver it.

*The sumptuous Eagle console, with a carved and gilded eagle reflected in a
mirror back, is made of sycamore inlaid with Madrona burr.*

The New England home of couturier Bill Blass dates from 1749.
Opposite and above right: The drawing room with its soothing grey-green
walls and ticking upholstery, displays a collection of classical objects
and furniture. The round Regency table was made for gaming, but the sofa,
suitably classical in design, dates from the 1930s. The walls are densely
hung with drawings and paintings.
Above left: A room for quiet contemplation, with library shelving
illuminated by angled brass lamps.

Above: A large bookcase holds an extensive library of handsomely bound volumes, still one of the most practical and sympathetic ways of displaying and storing books.

Opposite: The library as fitted room is shown in this splendidly appointed interior, with classically designed bookcases forming an inner wall enclosing the entire room and providing a rich, mellow backdrop.

Above: The blue and white of Chinese porcelain is the unifying theme of this elegant drawing room, with handsome mirrored secretaire bookcase, pale faux marble panelling and framed Eastern hanging.

Opposite: The graphic setting of a contemporary kitchen makes a surprisingly effective background for antique furniture. The monochromatic scheme - white marble and black slate tiled floor, black venetian blind, black unit fronts and off-white walls - provides visual coherence.

Above: The world of antiquity left a legacy of design and ornament which has remained astonishingly vigourous and powerful for thousands of years.

Opposite: A classic evocation of the eighteenth-century interior, with mellow painted panelled walls, Chippendale style chair and mahogany tripod tea table.

Left: The intimate charm of an eighteenth-century French boudoir is captured in this prettily decorated bedroom, with Georgian four-poster and comfortable seat furniture.

Right: The beautiful lines of classical furniture are emphasized by the quiet understatement of this interior, with its white walls, light toned carpet and evocative lighting (shown here in two views).

*Above: The curving lines of a Biedermeier sofa set against a luminous aquamarine wall.
Biedermeier was the domestic version of Empire style popular in Northern Europe in the early
decades of the nineteenth century.*

*Opposite: An eclectic blend of old and new creates an interior of appealing vitality and
interest, with classical elements relished for their decorative quality.*

Above: This setting at Castle Howard displays the drama of formal dining, with candlelight reflected in polished mahogany, glittering silver plate in the pedimented dresser, sparkling glassware and crisp linen.

Opposite: A tented ceiling makes a magnificent foil for the classical features of a central hall, with its striking design of columns and niches and ordered symmetries.

PICTURE ACKNOWLEDGEMENTS

Designs and photographs from David Linley Furniture are on pages 2(B), 4, 5, 6, 8, 11, 12, 13,(TR,BL), 14, 16, 17, 18, 19, 102, 104, 105, 110, 116, 117, 123, 124-125, 126(T), 130, 131, 140, 141 (T), 146(T), 150, 151(L), 159, 164, 173.

The black and white furniture designs throughout are from original pattern books:
Thomas Chippendale 'The Director'
Hepplewhite 'The Cabinet-Maker and Upholsterer's Guide' (Third Edition)
Thomas Sheraton 'The Cabinet-Maker and Upholsterer's Drawing-Book'
Ince and Mayhew 'The Universal System of Household Furniture'

Illustrations acknowledgements:

9: Fritz von der Schulenburg
10: The Royal Collection © 1993 Her Majesty the Queen
13(TL): Landscape Only/Christopher Joyce
15: Fritz von der Schulenburg
20: Scala
21: Scala/Casa di Paquio Proculo, Pompeii
22: British Architectural Library, RIBA, London
25: By courtesy of the Trustees of the Sir John Soane's Museum, London
27: Laing Art Gallery, Newcastle-upon-Tyne, Tyne and Wear Museums
28: Scala/Museo Etrusco, Tarquinia
29: Scala/Museo Nazionale, Naples
30: Scala/Accademia, Venice
31: Scala
32: Angelo Hornak/Courtauld Galleries, London
33: British Architectural Library, RIBA, London
34-35: Paolo Marton, Treviso
37: Angelo Hornak
38: Yale Center for British Art, Paul Mellon Collection
40: Courtesy of the Board of Trustees of the V&A, London
41: Christie's Images, London
42: Clay Perry
43: Fritz von der Schulenburg
44: Courtesy of the Board of Trustees of the V&A, London
45: Arcaid/Richard Bryant
46: Mary Evans Picture Library
47: Bridgeman Art Library/Towneley Art Gallery, Burnley
48: Christie's Images, London
50: Number One Royal Crescent, owned by Bath Preservation Trust
51: Angelo Hornak
53: John Bethell

54-55: John Bethell
56: By courtesy of the Trustees of the Sir John Soane's Museum, London
57: Arcaid/Richard Bryant
58: Monticello, Thomas Jefferson Memorial Foundation Inc
60: Toledo Museum of Art, Ohio: gift of an anonymous donor
63: By courtesy of the Museum of Fine Arts, Boston, Ellen Kelleran Gardner Fund
64: Arcaid/Richard Bryant
65: Courtesy of the Board of Trustees of the V&A, London
67: Angelo Hornak/Courtesy of the Board of Trustees of the V&A
71: Arcaid/Richard Bryant
72: Courtesy of the Board of Trustees of the V&A, London
74-75: Clay Perry
76(T): Courtesy of the Board of Trustees of the V&A, London
76-77: Spencer House/Mark Fiennes
78: Courtesy of the Board of Trustees of the V&A, London
79: Angelo Hornak/National Trust
80(T): Angelo Hornak/courtesy of the Harewood House Trust
80(B): Harewood House Trust
81(T): Harewood House Trust
81(B): Temple Newsam House, Leeds City Art Galleries
82: Fritz von der Schulenburg
83,84: Fritz von der Schulenburg
89: John Bethell/Private Collection
90: Courtesy of the Board of Trustees of the V&A, London
91: Christie's Images, London
92: Musées Nationaux, Paris
93: The Metropolitan Museum of Art, New York, Rogers Fund, 1933
95: Musées Nationaux, Paris/Musée du Louvre
96: Courtesy of the Board of Trustees of the V&A, London
97: The Metropolitan Museum of Art, New York, John Stewart Kennedy Fund 1918
98: Courtesy, Winterthur Museum, Delaware
99(T): Courtesy, The Winterthur Library: Joseph Downs Collection of Manuscripts and Printed Ephemera
99(B): Courtesy, Winterthur Museum, Delaware
100: The Metropolitan Museum of Art, Rogers Fund, 1915
101: The Metropolitan Museum of Art, New York, Purchase, Gifts of Mrs Russell Sage and various other donors, 1969
108(TL): Courtesy of the Board of Trustees of the V&A, London

108(TC): John Bethell/by courtesy of the Marquess of Zetland
108(TR): Mallett & Son (Antiques) Ltd, London
109(TR): Bridgeman Art Library/Mallett & Son (Antiques) Ltd, London
109(BL,BR): Courtesy of the Board of Trustees of the V&A, London
111(T): The Trustees of the Sir John Soane's Museum, London
112(T): Bridgeman Art Library/Mallett & Son (Antiques) Ltd, London
113(B): Angelo Hornak/Courtesy of the Board of Trustees of the V&A
114: Christie's Images, London
115(T): Christie's Images, London
115(B): Courtesy of the Board of Trustees of the V&A, London
118(R): Christie's Images, London
119(TL): Mallett & Son (Antiques) Ltd, London
119(R): Christie's Images, London
120(L): Courtesy of the Board of Trustees of the V&A, London
120(TR): Christie's Images, London
120(BR): Mallett & Son (Antiques) Ltd, London
121: Christie's Images, London
123(L): Angelo Hornak/National Trust
127(L,BR): Mallett & Son (Antiques) Ltd, London
128(TL): Christie's Images, London
128-129: Christie's Images, London
132(T): Mallett & Son (Antiques) Ltd, London
132(B): Courtesy of the Board of Trustees of the V&A, London
133(L): Christie's Images, London
133(BR): Angelo Hornak
135: Christie's Images, London
138(L): Courtesy of the Board of Trustees of the V&A, London
138(R): The Metropolitan Museum of Art, Gift of Mrs Russell Sage, 1909. Photograph by Richard Cheek
139(L): Mallett & Son (Antiques) Ltd, London
141(B): Fritz von der Schulenburg
142(L): Mallett & Son (Antiques) Ltd, London
142(TR): Courtesy of the Board of Trustees of the V&A, London
142-143: Mallett & Son (Antiques) Ltd, London
143(TR): Bridgeman Art Library/Bonhams, London
143(B): Courtesy of the Board of Trustees of the V&A, London
144(BL): Angelo Hornak

144(R): Courtesy of the Board of Trustees of the V&A, London
145(L): Mallett & Son (Antiques) Ltd, London
146(B): By courtesy of the Marquess of Cholmondeley
147: By courtesy of the Trustees of the Sir John Soane's Museum, London
148(L): Musées Nationaux, Paris/Musée de Malmaison
149(R): Courtesy of the Board of Trustees of the V&A, London
151(R): Courtesy of the Board of Trustees of the V&A, London
152(T,B): Courtesy of the Board of Trustees of the V&A, London
153(L): Angelo Hornak
156: Christie's Images, London
156(R): Courtesy of the Board of Trustees of the V&A, London
157(L,R): Christie's Images, London
158: Arcaid/Richard Bryant
160: Royal Academy
163: Musées Nationaux, Paris/Chateau de Malmaison
165: Fritz von der Schulenburg
167: Robert Harding Picture Library/Michael Jenner
168-169: Christopher Simon Sykes
170,171: Christopher Simon Sykes
172: Arcaid/Niall Clutton
174: Fritz von der Schulenburg
175(L,R): Fritz von der Schulenburg
176-180: Fritz von der Schulenburg
180-181: Elizabeth Whiting Associates/June Buck
182: Robert Harding Picture Library/IPC Magazines/James Merrell
183(T,B): Elizabeth Whiting Associates/Andreas von Einsiedel (Designer Gerard Conway)
184: Fritz von der Schulenburg
185: Henry Bourne
186, 187: Fritz von der Schulenburg

Front jacket

TL: Arcaid/Richard Bryant
TR: Angelo Hornak/by courtesy Harewood House Trust
BC: David Linley Furniture
BR: Angelo Hornak

Back jacket

TL: Courtesy of the Board of Trustees of the V&A
TR: David Linley Furniture
BL: Angelo Hornak/by courtesy Harewood House Trust

INDEX